UNITED
AIRLINES

SIMON FORTY

PLYMOUTH PRESS

IAN ALLAN
Publishing

First published 1997

ISBN 0 7110 2531 2

Published by Ian Allan Publishing

An imprint of Ian Allan Ltd, Terminal House, Station Approach, Shepperton, Surrey TW17 8AS.
Printed by Ian Allan Printing Ltd at its works at Coombelands in Runnymede, England.

Code: 9710/B

CONTENTS

Front cover: *Boeing 727-222 N770UA at London Heathrow.* Austin J. Brown

Back cover: *Boeing 777-400.* Austin J. Brown

Below: *The delivery ceremony for United's first Boeing 777 took place on 17 May 1997. It entered revenue service with United on 7 June, the inaugural flight being between London Heathrow and Washington.* Boeing

Acknowledgements
Thanks to all those who helped with this project, specifically the United UK Press Office, Peter Waller, Nick Grant, Jonathan and Sandra Forty, Philip Birtles, Austin Brown, Günter Endres, Peter March and Leo Marriott.

Introduction

Through nearly seven decades United Airlines has steadily built itself up into the largest United States carrier and the second largest aviation business in the world. The company's origins go right back to 1926 when brave young pilots flew open-cockpit biplanes across the near-empty skies to deliver the US mail. Times have changed beyond the wildest speculations of those pioneer aviators; the same skies are now studded with aircraft of all descriptions — many of them belonging to United Airlines.

The company grew from humble beginnings after merging four pioneering US carriers — Boeing Air Transport, National Air Transport, Pacific Air Transport and Varney Air Lines, until it became the vast business that today flies nearly nine million travellers on 70,000 international flights each year. Yet, surprisingly, this huge company did not fly outside the continent of North America until as recently

as 1983 when it was at last granted a transpacific licence to fly to Tokyo. From there its market has expanded out to the Pacific rim to encompass the ever-expanding Asiatic economies, and in the opposite direction across the Atlantic to tap the lucrative markets that western Europe offers. South America is also now on the United network, leaving only Africa and the former Soviet Union states as gaps on its globe.

As one of the earliest and hungriest airline companies United Airlines can boast many aviation 'firsts': in 1927, in the earliest days of passenger travel, it was the first company to offer a coast-to-coast service. Two years later United helped make a colossal step forward in aviation safety when it was the first to develop and adopt a practical system of ground-to-air two-way radio communication. In 1930, United trialled the first air stewardesses and in 1936 it was the first to have its own flight

Below: *Boeing 777-222 N770UA at London Heathrow, January 1997. United spent four years working closely with Boeing helping to create the 777's baseline design.* Austin J. Brown

kitchen to make and provide meals for passengers in-flight. In 1955 United Airlines was the first to fly nonstop New York-San Francisco and two years later it was the first transcontinental airline to be equipped with radar, soon to be a standard feature on every flightdeck.

A milestone was reached in 1964 when United became the first airline to fly more than one billion revenue passenger-miles in a single month. That same year it was the first carrier to install and operate a fully automatic, all-weather landing system which allowed its DC-8s to land in reduced visibility when ceilings were as low as 150ft. It became the first airline to exceed $1 billion revenue in a single year, in 1967. In 1990 United was the first commercial carrier to use satellite data communications in-flight. This allowed quick and clear uninterrupted communications between the cockpit and ground controllers.

Originally only active as a management company, United Airlines has consumed all its individual aviation purchases to emerge as a corporate entity to rival the best services in the world. The majority shareholders in the company are its own 82,000 employees who hold 55% of the stock, while United Airlines itself is a wholly-owned subsidiary of the UAL Corporation.

United Airways annually moves 75 million travellers across the skies on 2,200 daily departures from 140 airports in 30 countries around the world; nearly nine million of these passengers are on 70,000 international flights annually. In 1995 this earned United Airlines revenue of $14,943 million. Furthermore, United's cargo business has been on the increase, and in 1995 it moved 525,000 tonnes. The average age of aircraft in its fleet in 1995 was 10.7 years.

The company's world headquarters are at 1200 E. Algonquin Road, Elk Grove Township, Illinois 60007. Their mailing address is: UAL Corporation, PO Box 66100, Chicago, IL 60666, and United Airlines, PO Box 66100, Chicago, IL 60666.

Left: *The tail fin of a Boeing 777-222 in United colours juts out from behind the Boeing chalet at the Paris Air Show, Le Bourget, June 1995 less than a month after United had taken possession of its first 777.* Austin J. Brown

Right: *As a contrast, two years later, here is the similarly painted tail of 777-222 N770UA at London Heathrow in January 1997. United flies 777s to Heathrow from Chicago, Newark and Washington (Dulles).* Austin J. Brown

History

Although now one of the largest passenger carriers in the world, United Airlines originated, like most other American airlines, as a humble air-mail carrier. The US Post Office was a government authority which started the public mail service in May 1919 with veteran planes and pilots from the United States Army Signal Corps. By 1923 operations were on a sounder footing and had become more professional, this in turn allowing pilot life expectancy to increase from a lowly four years. By the following year, the US mail could fly from east to west coast (or vice versa) in just 32hr. A massive reduction from the previous 82hr that the former rail and plane service achieved.

In 1925 the US Congress authorised the Postmaster General to call for bids from private operators to fly the mail routes; this in turn led to the formation of new aviation companies eager to compete for the lucrative routes. One such bidder was Vern Gorst, the boss of Pacific Air Transport. His enthusiasm for the new technology of flight drove him to considerable achievements, and his company would, in time, grow to become one of the main elements of the United system. By 1926 Pacific was able to offer passengers a seat on the Los Angeles-Seattle mail run for $132. Another pioneer who also chased the valuable Post Office contracts, was a World War 1 Army flyer Walter T. Varney, whose tiny company, Varney Air Lines, on 6 April 1926, was the first of the passenger lines that merged to become United to begin an air-mail service.

A third element and the key link in the evolution of United, was Boeing Air Transport, formed in specific response to the Post Office contracts by Bill Boeing, the aviation enthusiast and plane maker. His company was equipped with his own latest design: the Boeing 40-A mail plane. Costing $25,000 apiece, they were vastly superior in speed and performance to anything else around in the air at the time, and marked a milestone in air transportation history.

In late October 1928, the struggling Pacific Air Transport company was merged with Boeing Air Transport and Pratt & Whitney to become the United Aircraft & Transport Corporation. Shortly after acquiring Pacific Air Transport, W. A. Patterson, the company's financial adviser, was recruited to Boeing, and by the winter of the following year, following the sudden death of founder member Eddie Hubbard, he became operating head of the company.

Another vital component in the United system was Stout Air Services, bought by the United Aircraft & Transport Corporation in 1929 and later merged into National Air Transport. Backed by Henry and Edsel Ford, of Ford Motor Company fame, William B. Stout had launched the Stout Metal Airplane company. Stout — a mechanical genius — revolutionised plane design by abandoning the usual materials of spruce and canvas and instead presenting a machine constructed entirely of metal. This became the Ford Tri-motor plane, nicknamed 'The Tin Goose' by its pilots. With this plane, which was able to take off on a short runway, the Fords won the Dearborn-Chicago/Cleveland air-mail contract. Stout Air Services also won the Detroit-Grand Rapids air-mail contract, and supplemented the service by carrying passengers between Detroit-Cleveland, and Detroit-Chicago.

The late 1920s and early 1930s was an era of consolidation, and other big mergers were beginning to challenge the United Aircraft & Transport Corporation. One of its principal rivals was the Keys Group, which had bought into Varney Air Lines via its North American Aviation Corporation; it was also backing Maddux Air Lines, the western end of Transcontinental Air Transport, in an extension from Los Angeles-Seattle which corresponded with Boeing's Pacific Air Transport division.

Thus the holding company United Aircraft & Transport Corporation was created linking four companies: the Boeing Airplane Company, Boeing Air Transport, Pacific Air Transport, and Pratt & Whitney, the aircraft engine plant that produced the Wasp engine that powered the Boeing planes, owned by Fred Renschler. Renschler traded ownership of Pratt & Whitney for shares in and the presidency of the new concern.

The Hamilton Propeller Company, and later the Standard Steel Propeller Company were also acquired, along with Stearman Aircraft (makers of light aircraft), Northrop Aircraft (specialising in military trainers), the Sikorsky Airplane works (leaders in the field of flying boats — considered essential to any overseas operations), and two airport subsidiaries in California and Connecticut. Such a varied collection of aviation holdings each able to supply and support the other was recognised as the way forward to the future. United was now the largest air group in the United States of America.

Original Companies

Varney Air Lines: Founded by Walter T. Varney, an ex-war pilot Varney Air Lines was the first permanent holder of a US mail service contract from Pasco (Washington)-Boise (Idaho)-Elko (Nevada), a route of 460 miles, awarded in 1925. (By June the south-eastern terminus was changed to Salt Lake City.) First mail flight service was flown on 6 April 1926. September 1929 extended their operations to fly Pasco-Spokane-Portland-Seattle. Bought out in June 1930 by United Aircraft & Transport Corporation.

Pacific Air Transport: The company was organised and set up by Vern Gorst, a true aviation pioneer, in January 1926,

with a stable of 10 pilots and not enough money. Began air-mail service to points between Los Angeles and Seattle on 15 September 1926. Bought by Boeing Air Transport in January 1928 and became a member of the holding company, Boeing Airplane & Transport Corporation, although Pacific continued to operate as a separate division.

National Air Transport: Incorporated in Delaware on 21 May 1925 and claimed to be the first company to be founded specifically as an airline. The founder, Clement M. Keys, was a former *Wall Street Journal* financial editor. Began air-mail service on the 995-mile Chicago-Kansas City-Dallas route on 12 May 1926. In April 1927, won the Chicago-New York mail contract, first run in September 1927. Clement M. Keys lost control of the company to United Aircraft & Transport Corporation in March 1930 after bitter stock battles.

Boeing Air Transport: Founded by Bill Boeing. Began as a San Francisco-Chicago service in 1927, a 1,918-mile route. (The route was originally awarded to the Boeing Airplane Company who transferred it to Boeing Air Transport within three months.) In July 1927 started the San Francisco to Chicago mail service with 25 Wasp-powered Boeing 40s. In January 1928 bought Pacific Air Transport and merged completely in December the same year. Became Boeing Airplane & Transport Corporation as a holding company for the Boeing Airplane Company, Boeing Air Transport and Pacific Air Transport in October 1928. On 1 February 1929 formed the holding company United Aircraft & Transport Corporation after acquiring Pratt & Whitney and Pacific Air Transport.

Pratt & Whitney Aircraft Company: An old machine-building company in

Hartford, Connecticut, taken over in 1925 and developed by Frederick D. Renschler into an innovative engine developing and making company. Designed and built the epoch-making Wasp air-cooled radial engine, primarily intended for naval fighter planes but also put into Boeing Air Transport planes, giving them a colossal edge. Was amicably bought by the Boeing Airplane Company as a logical extension to their aircraft-building business in 1929.

All became (with the exception of Varney and National Air Transport) — **United Aircraft & Transport Corporation** on 1 February 1929. National Air Transport was incorporated into the group in March 1930 and Varney Air Lines joined three months later.

On 1 July 1931 United Airlines was organised as a management company for Boeing Air Transport, Pacific Air Transport, National Air Transport and Varney Air Lines.

The next consideration was for a single cross-country connection, and competition was fierce. The Keys Group had moved into Boeing's bailiwick with investments in Varney Air Lines and Western Air Express, and United's intention to reciprocate eastwards to New York sparked a 'battle of the giants'. Renschler tried to acquire National Air Transport, but soon came up against Clement M. Keys, the ubiquitous aviation promoter who had raised the money in New York and Chicago to found his own airline in 1925, and who refused to consider a merger. Renschler eventually acquired one third of NAT's shares through an exchange-of-stock agreement with various NAT shareholders. There followed a series of moves and ripostes from Keys, who outmanoeuvred Renschler when he got the directors of NAT to issue new share stock which was exchanged for North American Aviation shares, and had himself

elected as president of the airline. Renschler turned to the courts, and was able to prevent the issue of the new share stock, while his financial agent Joseph Ripley was busy acquiring more NAT shares — by purchase outright, or in exchange for United stock — ultimately leaving Renschler in control of 57% of NAT's stock. Finally, on 7 May, United formally took over NAT, which meant that it could at last offer a San Francisco-Chicago-New York run and thus the coveted 'Main Line' coast-to-coast operation.

In May 1930 Postmaster General Walter Brown summoned airline operators to a 'spoils conference' and soon afterwards he put into practice a new government policy to stimulate the airline industry further by helping to set up three continental rivals for United, while at the same time restricting United's attempts at growth. By the end of his period in office (1933), he had overseen the creation of 27,062 miles of airways, with the United system carrying 40% of all traffic.

Also in May 1930, Boeing Air Transport (by now a subsidiary of United Aircraft & Transport Corp) made aviation history by introducing flight attendants on its planes for a three-month trial. Until this time the passengers had been looked after — or not — by the pilot and co-pilot of the plane. The very first stewardess was a nurse from Cresco, Iowa, called Ellen Church, whose idea it was to initiate in-flight service using nurses who would be able to cope with any sickness problems, as well as provide food and drinks. Eight stewardesses (actually nurses) were engaged against the better judgement of Boeing management to serve on the 24hr flight between San Francisco-Chicago in a 12-passenger Boeing 80-A. They wore a smart uniform of dark green double-breasted jacket and skirt, a green cape with grey collar and silver buttons and green beret. They quickly became a success with passengers and crew alike as well as with Boeing management, and at the end of the trial period 20 more nurses were hired.

In July 1931 a new management company, United Airlines Inc, was created to oversee and co-ordinate the four separate commercial airlines. It did not own any of the planes or equipment, signed no contracts with the companies and had no earnings, but it was supported by the four member airlines. This move was to prove of immense value later on, when the emerging airlines were subject to government legislation. United first of all bought Stout Air Services for $175,000 and merged their small fleet of Ford Tri-motors into the National Air Transport set-up. Varney Air Lines then filled the seat of Stout as the fourth airline in the United Airlines hierarchy in June 1930, when it was eventually bought for $2 million. The merger of Boeing and NAT in the summer of 1930 shuffled the cards again. The New York Main Line became the first coast-to-coast airline under one management, using NAT-Boeing planes to carry three-quarters of the country's air mail, and a third of the country's passengers. Thus the United Airlines system became the first real transport giant.

By 1931, when W. A. Patterson became General Manager, the United network radiated from Chicago in all directions — 1,900 miles west to the Pacific coast, 750 miles east to the Atlantic, and 995 miles south to Dallas. United flew the Main Line carrying the bulk of the country's air traffic. The system's passenger business had tripled to 42,930 travellers; in 1932 it doubled to 88,935; then leaped to 127,695 in 1933. During this period United was developing increasing technical expertise, and with the capabilities of men like Thorp Hiscock and Russ Cunningham, solutions to various problems were found — including, crucially, two-way communication from ground to air, automatic piloting, de-icers for the wings of planes, fuel

temperature control, propeller pitch control, 'riding the beam' — using directional radio beams to aid navigation, solving the problem of radio interference — static, (caused by the planes themselves as they flew), and the development of recording barographic flight analysers — prototype Black Boxes. The 'romantic era' of solo flying had well and truly ended, being replaced by a much more professional and technological team approach.

In June 1932 construction began on the Boeing 247. United took delivery of its first Boeing 247 — the prototype of the modern airliner — to take passengers across America. This all-metal, twin-engined low wing aircraft came into service in June 1933 and quickly became a fleet of 30 planes. Each plane could take 10 passengers and the following year it reduced coast-to-coast flying time to 19hr and 30min. The principal stops were Los Angeles-San Francisco-Salt Lake City-Chicago-Cleveland-New York.

On 1 May 1934 Boeing Air Transport, National Air Transport, Pacific Air Transport and Varney Air Lines became a separate business entity called United Airlines. That same year saw the dropping of a stunning bombshell — the cancellation of all air-mail contracts by Postmaster General Farley. These contracts had been the life-blood of the growing airlines, and some small concerns consequently reduced their operations to mere token flights. But abrupt though the cancellations were, and despite being worth 45% of its business, United chose to keep flying, and was soon losing $1,000,000 a quarter. The government still needed the mail delivered and drafted in the Army to do the task; however, this contingency proved disastrous, and so the government recontracted the mail routes out, after first insisting on a purge of all who had attended Postmaster Brown's 'spoils conference' (with the inference of collusion).

In July 1934 William A. ('Pat') Patterson

became chief executive of the reorganised United Airlines (Boeing Air Transport, Pacific Air Transport, National Air Transport and Varney Air Lines), while continuing as vice-president of the operating company, United Airlines Inc. He had started his career as a Wells Fargo Bank officer in San Francisco, but became involved with the youthful airline business when he came into professional contact with Pacific Air Transport after they sought a $5,000 loan which he granted — this rash move was considered by his bosses as very high risk. He resigned from the Wells Fargo Bank in April 1929 to become an assistant at Boeing. His career in the airline business blossomed and he was to take United from its early pioneering days right through to the jet age by the time he retired in 1966.

The date 12 June 1934 saw Congress pass a new Air Mail Act; in essence this forbade airlines and plane manufacturers from being affiliated, including the banning of directors being in both camps and holding stocks in both businesses. This move was directly aimed at United who enjoyed a happy working relationship within the company between the Boeing aircraft factories and their airlines. Furthermore, the Act forbade salaries over $17,500 for executives sitting on the boards of companies holding mail contracts.

Overnight United Airlines had become an illegal organisation and was given five and a half months to resolve its structure to come into line with government dictates. Crisis meetings were held and fairly quickly the decision arrived at was to circumvent the Act altogether by splitting the United Aircraft & Transport holding company, worth $30,000,000, into three new operating companies. United Aircraft Corporation (comprising Pratt & Whitney, Sikorsky and Vought factories) took 51% of the assets.

Below: *From 247 to 777 — United and Boeing have been partners for many years: the companies that made up United bought a total of 70 Boeing 247s which entered service in 1933. Here a 247D is lined up with Boeing's latest aircraft, the 777.* United Airlines

The Boeing Airplane Company took 14½% of the holding company's assets and hived off on its own to run aircraft factories in Seattle and Wichita. Finally, United Airlines Transport Corporation (comprising the four airlines: National Air Transport, Pacific Air Transport, Varney and Boeing Air Transport, the Boeing School of Aeronautics and Burbank airport) were allocated 34½% of the holding company's resources. Through the auspices of the restructuring it was left debt-free with a working capital of $4,000,000. The separate identities of the four airlines were merged and their names dropped.

The following year United began the 'Long Suit', filing a claim for damages incurred after air-mail contract cancellations and to clear its executives of collusion charges. (It was eventually exonerated in 1943, and awarded token damages of $368,525.) The air-mail cancellations, as the government had intended, had forced the airlines to increase both passenger and cargo operations. In 1933 United's passenger revenue, $3,955,622 for 68,984,770 passenger-miles flown, constituted 40% of the airline's income. On 1 July the following year United began services to Canada. By 1935 the revenue figures showed $4,933,376 for 83,473,000 passenger-miles, and in 1936 the company topped the 100,000,000 passenger-mile mark, with income of $5,844,331 from passenger fares — almost 58% of the airline's total income.

United pushed its infant cargo business too, concluding a deal with the Railway Express Agency, to pick up and deliver cargo handled by United Airlines. However, United soon found itself in conflict with rival airlines who, thinking that Railway Express would generate business for the railways and not the air companies, organised General Air Express. This proved an expensive pick-up and delivery service which was only available in the larger cities anyway; consequently the business did not run for long before the other airlines came round and were ready to join United in negotiating a new blanket contract with the Railway Express Agency. Although United's earnings from Express were relatively small, the figures showed an impressive gain: in 1933, $133,153 flying 184,285 ton-miles of air express, by 1936, working with Railway Express, it earned $431,653 flying 760,000 ton-miles of air express — only 4.27% of total income, but the start of much bigger things.

During this period (1934-7) United was overtaken as the industry's largest carrier by American Airlines, which had worked hard to double the number of population centres reached by its system. American's direction was taken to counter United's decision to develop intensively its Main Line territory — the historic overland route from coast to coast. United's decision in turn was forced because the company was still heavily out of favour with the government, with whom it was still embroiled in the 'Long Suit'. Throughout this period United got nowhere with its applications for new routes, so instead the company worked to integrate its system still further by developing feeder lines for in-depth coverage of existing routes.

To make life even harder, the government granted its arch rivals, TWA and American Airlines, certificates to fly on United's heaviest and most lucrative traffic route, namely New York-Chicago; American flying via Detroit and Buffalo, and TWA via Pittsburgh. One small acquisition was accomplished: the purchase of the Cheyenne-Denver route plus air-mail contract, from Wyoming Air Services for $209,000. This connected Denver to the Main Line, a situation its residents had petitioned to achieve for a long time. A minor victory against a hostile government, the purchase became hugely important a few years down the line when Denver unexpectedly became the heart of the United system.

At this time both TWA and American were flying the Chicago-New York route using the Douglas DC-3; faster than the Boeing 247 that United used. The DC-3 could make the journey nonstop, whereas the 247 had to refuel at Cleveland. When United switched to DC-3s at the end of 1936, the incredibly sturdy 247s were not sold but used instead on the feeder routes that intensified the air coverage in United's system. In this time of government disapproval and intense competition, United's profits took a heavy pounding, barely breaking even in 1935, and only $371,000 in 1936. (It was not until 1938 that the Civil Aeronautics Act emancipated the airlines from government control.) To counteract this financial decline, United executives came up with numerous imaginative schemes to attract passengers from rival airlines — the first flight kitchens for the preparation of in-flight meals were established in Oakland, California, in December 1936; an overnight sleeper service on the coast-to-coast route in 1937; and in the same year luxury lounges called 'Skylounge' on the New York-Chicago service, plus loyalty ticket rebates and free spouse tickets.

These inducements worked well for a time and increased passenger traffic, but following a series of tragic plane crashes, passengers left the air in their thousands. W. A. Patterson's response was to bring in an air safety expert, 'Shorty' Schroeder, and to increase the company's share stock to raise $4,000,000 for the next step in aircraft development in conjunction with Douglas which would bring the industry into the jet age: the four-engined Douglas DC-4. As other airlines heard of this project they asked to be counted in, and soon United, Transcontinental & Western, Pan Am , Eastern and American Airlines were all involved in the collaboration, though it was not for long. Costs were high, and the agreement by all participants to buy no other plane in its class was circumvented

by Pan Am and Eastern, who ordered the new four-engined pressurised Boeing Stratoliner, 1,000lb under the 50,000lb limit.

In 1940 United became the first airline to provide all-cargo flights, just in time as it transpired, with war in Europe looking increasingly likely. But meanwhile in 1940, the airlines were increasingly important in the movement of national defence passenger and cargo traffic, and by the end of the year the Boeing School of Aeronautics had begun teaching military personnel.

Back in 1939 United had test flown and ordered the DC-4, but before Douglas could start production, Robert A. Lovett, the Assistant Secretary of War, summoned W. A. Patterson to inform him that war was not far off, and that the DC-4 was just what was needed for service in the United States Air Force. So, in 1941, United cancelled their order, American Airlines followed suit, and the DC-4 became the Douglas Skymaster, the aerial workhorse of the war. By the time Douglas was free to build the commercial version in 1945, three new faster and larger airliners had emerged as a result of the wartime increase in aeronautical design and technological development. These were the Boeing Stratocruiser, the Douglas DC-6, and the Lockheed Constellation.

After giving up the DC-4s the airlines, under the guidance of Edgar S. Gorell, made plans for the pooling of resources to form a global war transport system. This sounded altruistic but its primary aim was to avoid being taken over by the government. On 7 December Pearl Harbor was attacked by the Japanese and the US went to war. The following year United's overhaul base at Cheyenne became a modification centre for bombers, and airline operations began to Alaska and the Pacific under Army contract. In 1942 United turned over more than half of its fleet of 69 aeroplanes to the US Army specifically for the transpacific and Alaskan networks.

In 1943 the 'Long Suit' was finally

Above: *Douglas DC-6A N37591* Cargoliner San Francisco *was delivered to United on 13 April 1956 and would serve until February 1968.* via Günter Endres

Below: *DC-3A N16070D is nearing completion after restoration to her original United Airlines finish in 1987. Delivered on 25 November 1936 as* City of Reno, *N16070D operated United's inaugural New York-Chicago flight.* Robert S. Ellis

settled, with United awarded withheld airmail pay for all former subsidiary airlines. In June the Civil Aeronautics Board (CAB) award United the Toledo-Washington route, and the company also acquired 75% of stock in Lineas Aereas Mexicanas, SA. Coast-to-coast Cargoliner services were also begun towards the end of the year. In 1944 United applied for more routes, from San Francisco and Los Angeles to Honolulu, Cleveland-Hartford-Boston, and Detroit; and concluded over two and a half years' military flying in Alaska for the Air Transport Command.

In 1945 the war finally ended and United received a special National Safety Council Award for more than one billion accident-free passenger-miles. Bomber operations finished at Cheyenne, 5,500 Flying Fortresses having being prepared and sent out for combat. Furthermore, the Boeing School of Aeronautics could boast of its war contribution of having trained and graduated more than 7,000 military personnel.

The war had helped usher in the age of flight, the era of the passenger train was coming to an end and foreign travel no longer had to be by slow boat, as the public in general were now happily accepting the aeroplane as an everyday means of transportation. Furthermore, a wealth of aeronautical experience had been accumulated from the huge globe-circling operations of the armed forces and such expertise could be applied in the commercial sphere, improving standards of machinery, technology, engineering and flying skills. In 1946, 12,000,000 people wanted to fly, but with so many air crews and planes still requisitioned by the military, there was great upheaval and disruption as the airlines struggled vainly to cope with the spectacular surge in demand. Even converted Army C-45s were used in an attempt to relieve congestion, but it was some time before the airlines recovered equipment and personnel from the military

and got back into the flow of commercial life. In truth the airlines had begun the war as small businesses, and finished it much bigger concerns.

In 1947 the first postwar airliner, the Douglas DC-6, flew coast-to-coast nonstop in 10hr. United acquired more routes and opened its San Francisco-Honolulu service on 1 May with a DC-6 Mainliner 300 seating 44 passengers. The flight took 10hr and cost $270 for the round trip, landing to great celebrations in Honolulu.

As ever at the forefront of aviation technology, the following year United was leading the field in design for centralised control of airline activities when it opened an operations hub at Denver. Then United concentrated all maintenance facilities in a new 'push-button' overhaul base at San Francisco. New advances in electronic navigation aids including Instrument Landing System (ILS) and surveillance radar were bringing greater dependability to airline operations. United's Family Air Travel plan proved popular and, on 8 July, United carried its 10 millionth passenger and flew its five billionth passenger-mile.

In 1950 the Boeing Stratocruiser service was introduced on the San Francisco-Honolulu route, and later that year United began its Los Angeles-Honolulu service. The year 1951 marked a quarter century of commercial air transportation for United Airlines, with the company ordering 55 of the new twin-engined Convair-Liner 340, and inaugurating its coast-to-coast service with four-engined DC-4 Mainliners.

The next year United continued its expansion with an order for 30 twin-engined Convair-Liner 340s for $16.5 million and 25 four-engined DC-7s. The Convair order was subsequently increased to 55. This enabled United to introduce a Mainliner Convair service to improve access to intermediate cities along the Main Line and with the four-engine DC-4 Mainliner, United were able to offer 66 passengers at a time a coast-to-coast

The McDonnell Douglas DC-8 was launched in 1955 and the first DC-8-10 entered service with United on 18 September 1959. McDonnell Douglas

service in 14hr, flying at a speed of 230mph. In 1953 United, in conjunction with the Radio Corporation of America, launched a programme to develop airborne radar for weather mapping on commercial transport; inaugurated DC-6 air coach flights flying California-Hawaii (which were then extended to cover the company's mainland routes); and opened a new centralised system control operating base at Denver. It also concluded three years of contract military operations to Tokyo.

The year 1954 saw new DC-7 Mainliners help United clock an all-time high of 300,000 miles of flying daily, fly its 30 millionth passenger, and complete the year with the best safety record in aviation history: 35 million passengers safely over 20 billion miles.

To save the United States taxpayers spending unnecessary money on their air force, the government decided to compel national airlines to provide a standby airline fleet which could be called upon for service in times of crisis. Set up during the Korean War under a government national defence programme entitled the Civil Reserve Air Fleet (CRAF), 24 national airlines were on continuous standby to provide several hundred four-engined aircraft with crews for military use, ready within 48hr notice. For United this meant that almost a quarter of its planes had to be ready for long-range modification to enable them to fly overseas whenever called upon by the Department of Defense. In support of the planes, around 1,500 engineers and technicians were similarly on reserve.

In 1955 United completed the largest single airline financing programme in aviation history — $150,000,000 over five years for expansion into the jet age — placing its initial order on 25 October for 30 Douglas DC-8s costing $175 million. In May United began the first nonstop flights between New York-San Francisco with a flying time of only 8³/₄hr.

The company's employees passed the 20,000 mark in 1957, and the airline ordered 11 Boeing 720s and 10 additional DC-8s. Next year, 1958, saw the electronic reservations system RAMAC go on line, and United celebrating carrying its 50 millionth passenger. The company also began jet-flight crew training at Denver, and the following year the first Douglas DC-8 Jet Mainliners were brought into service and shown to the public at Jetarama — a 12-month cross-country United Airlines promotional tour of 'the greatest airline show on earth' designed to introduce the American public to the idea of jet flight as opposed to prop-driven flight.

1960 was an important year for United Airlines: its first Boeing 720 jetliner was delivered and the company opened its new state-of-the-art terminal at New York International Airport. More aircraft orders were announced, this time 20 medium-range Caravelle jetliners from France which came into service in 1961. DC-7A Cargoliners were put into service on the freight side of the business. Plans were also announced for the merger of Capital Airlines with United, which was formally approved by the Civil Aeronautics Board and carried out the following year, on 1 June 1961. This was the largest merger in the history of the United States and made the company the biggest airline in the world excluding Aeroflot. It now served 116 cities with a fleet of 267 aircraft.

All this expansion meant that United had grown out of its current offices at Midway Airport and plans were made for a new complex on a 51-acre site, plus a new $2,000,000 Training Centre near Chicago's O'Hare Airport. United completed its first full year of jet service, carrying 1,300,000 passengers over more than 1,800,000,000 revenue passenger-miles.

In 1964 United became the first domestic carrier to install a fully automatic, all-weather landing system. This additional safety feature helped to consolidate its 'Fly the Friendly Skies' advertising campaign

Above: *Delivered in July 1960, United's 720-022 N7202U would serve until 1973. It was United's second Model 720 and the second built. United ordered 29 with services beginning on 5 July 1960.* Boeing

launched the following year.

The company became a wholly-owned subsidiary of a newly formed holding company, UAL Inc, in 1969, and the following year the holding company purchased Western International Hotels. In 1972 Instamatic, United's pioneering passenger reservation system which had been previewed at Jetarama and installed in 1961 was retired, and a new computer reservations system named Apollo came on line. By 1976 the company was offering travel agencies a computerised system for handling reservations.

The Airline Deregulation Act was passed in 1978, which called for the gradual closing down of CAB and its regulatory functions, freeing the airlines to price their own services and select their own routes. United's biggest block to global expansion was its lack of services beyond North America. Canada had been served since 1934 and Mexico came on line as late as 1980, but the company held no transpacific or Atlantic routes. For more than 17 years

United had been fruitlessly applying for non-domestic licences, until in 1983 it was finally granted permission to fly transpacific. United's first scheduled service outside the North American continent started on 1 April 1983, with a nonstop flight between the Pacific northwest-Tokyo. This was followed with a nonstop service from Seattle-Hong Kong. To cater for this new direction the company also established a west coast hub at San Francisco.

In August 1983, United took delivery of B-767-200s with which it strengthened its international services. Then, in 1984, United was proud to boast that now it had become the first airline to provide services to all 50 states belonging to the union of the United States.

UAL Inc completed its buy-out of the Hertz Corporation in 1985, and the following year managed the hugely important purchase of Pan Am's Pacific division for $715 million, on 7 February 1986. This gave United the right to fly scheduled services to an additional 11 prominent cities in 10

Above: *The Sud Aviation SE210 Caravelle was the first short-range aircraft designed with turbojets. United ordered 20 of the 6R version, which entered service in 1961.* Sud Aviation

Below: *DC-8-61 N8093U was delivered to United in October 1968 and would see service until 1991. In 1981 it was converted into a DC-8-70 — as were many Sixty series DC-8s — by re-engining with CFM56 turbofans.* Ian Allan Library

Above: *United DC-8-51 N8008U at Denver on 10 September 1979. The Series 50 was available as an updating kit or as new.* Wilfred C. Wann Jr

Below: *The first Boeing aircraft to be launched without a US customer (Lufthansa took the first), the 737 short/medium-range airliner would go on to become the most popular jet ever. United would be the launch customer for the 737-200, the first entering service in April 1968. Here, 737-22 N9021U is at Kansas City in August 1979.* Wilfred C. Wann Jr

Above: *Freight has always been significant to United. Here, a DC-8F takes on loaded pallets.* United Airlines

Below: *The Boeing 727 was another highly successful Boeing jet. 727-222 N7297U was the 1,500th 727 off the production line which would stop only after 1,831 had been built — a staggering total.* Boeing

Above: *United was the launch customer of the 727, another example of the close cooperation between Boeing and the company. Here, 727-22 N7056U at Kansas City in August 1979.* Wilfred C. Wann Jr

Below: *United Express-liveried Convair 580 N5823 was delivered in 1976. The 580 had Allinson 501 turboprops and this model passed from original owner Allegheny Airlines to Aspen Airways in 1976.* Peter R. March

Above: *Despite the airliner's early problems, United stuck with the DC-10 and it proved long-lived. DC-10-10 N1806U, delivered on 23 December 1972, served until 1994.* McDonnell Douglas

Pacific rim countries and gain direct access to the growing tiger economies there. In 1986 United began its new east coast hub operation at Washington DC's Dulles International Airport, and formed joint marketing ventures with the commuter airlines Air Wisconsin and Aspen and WestAir, creating United Express. This latter became the umbrella company under which the feeder services operated, taking passengers further and deeper into America than the main United services.

The year 1987 saw the company streamline and consolidate by selling off all its non-airline businesses. The next year United initiated a worldwide marketing partnership with British Airways, co-ordinating schedules, sharing facilities, one-stop check-ins and joint pricing, the intention being to give passengers easier access to more destinations, with simplified interchanges and fares. By 1988 the company had completed its massive restructuring, becoming the UAL Corporation, with United Airlines as its

principal subsidiary and main holding.

That same year United sold 50% of stoc of the Apollo reservation system to the Covia Partnership (including Alitalia, British Airways, KLM, Swissair and USAir). Midwa through the following year, United placed the largest aircraft order in aviation history, for 370 narrow-bodied and 32 wide-bodied aircraft. The company also announced it was to begin services to Europe, and became the first to offer 747-400 flights between the US and Australia and Hong Kong. In October 1996, United launched th world's longest nonstop scheduled service three times a week between Chicago and Hong Kong. The 7,789 mile flight took 16h by the 747-400. This meant that United ha become the largest transpacific carrier, surpassing all competitors.

The early 1990s were important years United Airlines as the company expanded to become a truly global carrier. The first step came in 1990 when United inaugurated services to Frankfurt from Chicago O'Hare and Washington DC's ulles airports. Then in the following year his move was further consolidated by the urchase of Pan Am's hub and other assets t London Heathrow. At a stroke, United ained six transatlantic and seven intra-urope routes to add to its growing etwork, and crucially, obtained invaluable nding rights at the busiest passenger irport in the world — London Heathrow. hen, in 1992, United flew into South merica with an initial service between liami-Caracas, Venezuela. Within six ionths this operation had expanded to 13 ties in 11 South American countries, iaking United one of the prime ternational carriers to serve the southern ontinent.

United claimed another aviation 'first' in 990 when it became the first carrier to take elivery of and fly the state-of-the-art oeing 777 aircraft. The world's first venue 777 flight was a United Heathrow-'ashington flight on 7 June 1995. This roved so successful that the plane took ver from the 747 on the transatlantic route ompletely and all 747 services to London ere discontinued. This enabled United to vive the flagship, globe-spanning Flight 1 hich operates Los Angeles-New York-ondon-Delhi-Hong Kong-Los Angeles. ight 2 follows the same route, but estbound.

ESOP

Employee Stock Ownership Plan — ESOP — was approved on 12 July 1994 by United's shareholders. This historic recapitalisation made United Airlines the argest majority employee-owned company in the world. By the year 2000 it s calculated that 55% of the ownership f UAL Corporation would be lodged in employees' accounts in the form of ESOP Preferred Shares. Furthermore, employees would gain representation on the board of directors, majority voting control of the company and job security provisions as well as other benefits.

ESOP is essentially a retirement plan for United's staff, the pilots, IAM-represented employees, US management and salaried employees. The idea behind the plan was to reduce United's costs, thus allowing the company to stay ultra-competitive against the smaller low-cost short-haul carriers who were hungry for United's domestic markets. This would be achieved by instigating changes in pay, benefit and working practices from the three participating employee groups.

United employees have primary voting control over all matters that affect the company's future — including, of course, any decisions on new purchases and mergers. A stipulation in the ESOP plan requires that as long as United employees own at least 20% of UAL Corporation stock, employees will continue to hold 55% of the voting rights. This situation is expected to pertain until 2016 at the earliest. In February 1996 nearly 3,800 of these shareholders were employed in 15 foreign countries who gained stock through international stock ownership programmes.

ESOP is administered by the State Street Bank of Boston. They also allocate ESOP Preferred Shares to employees' accounts during the Wage Investment Period which lasts until 2000. These shares earn a fixed dividend of $8.89 each year until 2000, which are paid in the form of additional shares of ESOP Preferred Stock. The shares are allocated in three distinct ways, two of which are tax qualified plans. This is so that shares can be given to each employee in such a way as to make the most of any tax incentives for which they qualify. For certain types of ESOP stock an employee, on leaving or retiring from the company, can elect to have the shares commuted into cash.

In May 1997 United announced the creation of 'Star Alliance', an integrated worldwide transport network in conjunction with Lufthansa, SAS, Air Canada and Thai Airways. The intention of the link-up was to provide better facilities for travellers flying beyond each network's destinations. For the passenger this would mean easier ticketing and smoother transfers between servers, plus other benefits. For the airlines, the attraction of the alliance lay in its ability to bring in more customers .

US exemption was granted recently in August 1996 to allow the proposed Lufthansa/United tie-up. The companies needed exemption from US anti-trust laws before the alliance could go ahead. However, the proviso that the government stipulated was that certain key routes, where the airlines are dominant, would be excluded from the agreement.

In November United announced more aircraft orders worth $3.5 billion to increase its already enormous fleet: 19 747s, two more 777s to bring the fleet up to 36, and six 757s. The 747s together with the 28 B-400s already on order or in service will increase United's fleet of Pratt & Whitney engined wide-bodies to 47.

In February 1997 United Airlines announced that it had reached two code-sharing agreements which, pending government approval, will allow a link-up with Air New Zealand on all flights between the United States and Australasia, and another code-share with Mexicana Airlines on flights between Mexico City and the United States. In April 1997 United introduced the first of its new long-range Boeing 777s with a twice daily, nonstop service between San Francisco-London

Heathrow. The 777s will replace the smaller Boeing 767 jets. Then, in June, United became the first airline to fly the Boeing 777 on scheduled flights between Washington DC-Heathrow, and since the GE90 powerplant was granted extended range approval, United Airlines has started to use the 777 on the long-haul Chicago-Heathrow services. Currently United Airlines, along with its major domestic rivals American Airlines, are the only US carriers with access to hugely profitable and accordingly highly valuable Heathrow landing slots.

Since United took over Pan Am's routes in 1991, it has become the largest US carrier at London Heathrow with 11 flights per day, including feeder services from Amsterdam and Brussels. (These also include Pan Am's transatlantic service to Paris and Frankfurt in 1990.)

Heathrow has become United's prime European gateway. Initially the company tried to emulate the familiar US-style hub and spoke system using ageing Boeing 727s to feed from points such as Berlin, Brussels and Munich. However, this proved too costly — requiring crew stay-over facilities and high operating costs, since the planes were kept on the ground for too long because of the airport's congested runways. Furthermore, it was discovered that passengers didn't like transferring from wide-bodied transatlantic planes to narrow-bodied jets. However, these feeder flights protected United's valuable landing slots, were worth continuing for that reason alone The solution lay in alliances with code-sharing partners, with Lufthansa eager to take some of the loss-making 727 routes. Currently United are fifth in size at Heathrow, and Lufthansa fourth largest.

United Airlines is fed at Heathrow by British Midland's UK network, Lufthansa flights from Germany and SAS in Scandinavia. Some traffic also comes in from the Emirates service to Dubai and Thai International's daily Bangkok flights. The slots once used for United's European

Above: *Launch customer with an order for 30, United's first 767 was delivered in August 1983. 767-222ER N607UA* City of Denver *was the second.* Austin J. Brown

services are now used for transatlantic routes. The alliances are considered to have worked well and seem to be winning more passengers as a result of the increasingly customer-friendly efforts put in to build up brand loyalty. One example of this is the recent introduction of an arrivals lounge for first and business class passengers, where, after their flight or during transfer, they can shower, dress, have coffee, etc. The all-round effort has paid off and in 1997 readers of *Executive Travel* magazine voted United 'Best Transatlantic Airline', the first time any US airline has won the award.

With this new venture, United has formed an Atlantic Division to manage its entire European operation from London, rather than from its Chicago headquarters. Today more than 2,500 employees are based in Europe — many of them local nationals — including 1,300 flight attendants domiciled in London, Paris and Frankfurt.

From early June 1997, JFK will be the only US airport with a daily year-round 767

(the smallest intercontinental aircraft) service from Heathrow — the most heavily travelled transatlantic route. This service is reckoned to be easy to make money on as a 'niche operation'. Flights are scheduled for a morning, a lunch time and an evening 767. Such frequency keeps the route profitable.

By 1997 United Airlines had become the largest majority employee-owned airline company as well as the largest carrier in the world. It flies more than 2,200 flights a day to 149 destinations in 30 countries. In all, the figures seem to be steadily increasing. Preliminary results for April 1997 were announced as follows: United flew 6,792,000 passengers on scheduled flights in April 1997; passenger miles had increased 4.8% compared to the same time in 1996; and cargo freight ton-miles had increased 26.6%. This last enormous rise the company ascribes to its extra Boeing 777s, most of which work the transatlantic markets, and the DC-10 freighters which do the same across the Pacific.

Above: *777-222 N766UA at London Heathrow, October 1995.* Austin J. Brown

Below: *DC-10-10 N1802U has been with United since the early 1970s. It is seen here at Washington in 1993.* Peter R. March

Above: *The Boeing 747-400 is recognised by the extended upper deck and drag-reducing wingtip winglets.* Austin J. Brown

Below: *747-123 N154UA was originally delivered to American Airlines in August 1970. United bought it in October 1987: it is still in service.* Austin J. Brown

Above: *N183UA, a Boeing 747-422, was delivered in April 1992. It is seen here over Hong Kong's Kai Tak airport.* Peter R. March

Below: *The Boeing 747 entered service in January 1970 and 747-123 N154UA is a long-lived example. Originally American Airlines' N9664, delivered in August 1970, United bought it in 1987.* Austin J. Brown

The Hubs

(All figures are from 1995)

CHICAGO

Total daily departures	529
United	421
United Express	108
Employees	16,639
Enplaned passengers in 1994 (millions)	14.6
Daily	39,942
Nonstop destinations	90
Domestic destinations	82
International destinations	8

(Frankfurt, London, Mexico City, Paris, San Juan, Tokyo, Toronto, Vancouver)

SAN FRANCISCO

Total daily departures	345
United	231
United Express	114
Employees	18,938
Enplaned passengers in 1994 (millions)	8.1
Daily	21,886
Nonstop destinations	45
Domestic destinations	33
International destinations	12

(Calgary, Hong Kong, London, Mexico City, Osaka, Paris, Seoul, Sydney, Taipei, Tokyo, Toronto, Vancouver)

DENVER

Total daily departures	422
United	265
United Express	157
Employees	7,703
Enplaned passengers in 1994 (millions)	7.4
Daily	20,313
Nonstop destinations	58
Domestic destinations	57
International destinations	1

(Calgary)

WASHINGTON DC (DULLES)

Total daily departures	280
United	82
United Express	198
Employees	5,210
Enplaned passengers in 1994 (millions)	2.9
Daily	7,945
Nonstop destinations	29
Domestic destinations	20
International destinations	9

(Amsterdam, Brussels, Frankfurt, London, Madrid, Mexico City, Milan, Paris, Zurich)

Above: *737-291 N998UA was delivered to Frontier Airlines in May 1982. United bought it in July 1985 — one of 24 737s bought from Frontier — and re-registered it in June 1986. Seen here at Washington Dulles Airport in 1993.* Peter R. March

Below right: *777-222 N773UA at Paris Le Bourget, June 1995.* Austin J. Brown

International Operations

EUROPE	
Destinations	Amsterdam, Brussels, Frankfurt, London, Madrid, Milan, Paris, Zurich
Employees	2,303
Aircraft types	747, 777, 767
Flights per day from the US	19
Number of intra-continental flights per day	1

PACIFIC		LATIN AMERICA	
Destinations	Bangkok, Beijing, Hong Kong, Manila, Osaka, Seoul, Shanghai, Singapore, Taipei, Tokyo, Delhi	Destinations	Belo Horizonte, Buenos Aires, Caracas, Guatemala City, Lima, Mexico City, Montevideo, Rio de Janeiro, San Jose, San Salvador, Santiago, Sao Paulo
Employees	2,123	Employees	943
Aircraft types	747, DC-10	Aircraft types	737, 747, 757, 767, A320
Flights per day from the US	21	Flights per day from the US	19
Number of intra-continental flights per day	11	Number of intra-continental flights per day	4

Below: *Boeing 747-422 N190UA was built in 1993 and is seen at Auckland airport, New Zealand.* Brian S. Strickland

Affiliated Companies

UNITED EXPRESS

The vastness of the domestic US market means that United Airlines has had to develop a feeder network of associate carriers who serve the regions under the United Express banner.

Atlantic Coast Airlines
Formed in December 1989 to bring passengers in from the 41 cities in the eastern United States to Washington DC. The headquarters offices are located at Sterling, Virginia. Its fleet consists of 29 BAe Jetstream 31/32s and 25 Jetstream 41s, with a further 11 on order.

Air Wisconsin Airlines Corporation
Now owned by CJT Holdings who bought the company in 1993 from United, it is still an important link in its services. Air Wisconsin feeds the Chicago and Denver hubs and is headquartered at Appleton, Wisconsin. Its fleet consists of 12 BAe 146-100/-200s.

Great Lakes Airlines
Founded on 25 October 1989, although it did not start services until 12 October 1981. It is located at Spencer, Iowa. Its fleet consists of 30 Beech 1900Cs, eight 1900Ds and 12 EMB-120ERs.

Mountain West
Part of the Mesa Air Group located at Farmington, New Mexico, the company was established in 1990. It feeds passengers from 71 cities into Albuquerque, Denver, Los Angeles and Phoenix.

Its fleet consists of 47 Beech 1900C/Ds, seven DHC-8-300s, and 10 EMB-120RTs.

United Feeder Service (UFS)
Headquartered at St Louis, Missouri. It operates primarily out of Chicago.

WestAir Commuter Airlines
Also part of the Mesa Air Group, this company was established in 1972 to feed passengers from 25 cities in Washington, Oregon and California into United hubs at Seattle, Portland, San Francisco and Los Angeles. The company is located in Fresno, California. Its fleet consists of 21 BAe Jetstream 31s, and 15 EMB-120RTs.

UNITED AIRLINES CARGO SERVICE

Headquartered in Chicago, a vital element in the United Airlines success story is its cargo division which by 1997 served 30 countries on five continents from eight US gateways, with a fleet of more than 550 aircraft. Alliances with foreign airlines through code-sharing agreements give it the world's largest cargo network. In 1994 revenue for this totalled $645 million, a 4% rise on the previous year.

In 1994 United flew 2 billion cargo ton-miles; most of this (around 77%) was freight, with mail making up the balance. The freight consists of everything from perishables such as fruit and vegetables, fresh fish and cut flowers, to textiles and clothing, various items of printed matter such as magazines and computer products, plus heavier industrial items such as car parts, machinery and aircraft parts. To cater for frozen freight, United provides refrigeration facilities at many of its airport facilities.

At the Chicago Cargo Sales and Service Center an internal automated information system is used to book and track shipments made across and around the world. This unique service is offered to customers as Cargo Plus 1, which allows shippers to check flight availability, book and track their shipments as well as keep running tabs on departure and arrival times, all from its own desk at work.

Above: *The Airbus A320 was certificated in February 1988 but had been a sales success before then with over 400 orders to its name. It is one of the few European airliners to compete in a market dominated by US manufacturers. A320-232 N408UA was delivered to United in March 1994.* Airbus Industrie via Aviation Picture Library

Below: *767-222ER seen over Heathrow on 16 August 1968.* Peter R. March

Above: *United Express's WestAir Commuter Airlines leased Shorts 360-100 N132DA from the end of 1984 until May 1990.* Austin J. Brown

Another service offered to keep customers right up to the minute with their shipments involves the Cargo EDI (Electronic Data Interchange) Network. This provides autogenerated shipment statistics to any shipper who is able to receive computer generated messages. It offers various services:

International Freight
Uses freighter main deck or lower deck cargo space, or on passenger planes, in the belly cargo holdings.

UA Worldwide Express
This service guarantees delivery on schedule for urgent freight on both large and small shipments.

Small Package Dispatch (SPD)
Provides airport to airport delivery within the US on a next flight basis for packages weighing up to 70lb. Pick-up and delivery is also available.

First Freight
A premium flight specific shipping service which gets the freight as priority cargo on any domestic United flight. This tends to include live animals and perishables.

UA 2-Day
A US-only service for most city pairs, which guarantees delivery by 08.00 on the second day (in most markets) provided the package was delivered before midnight.

In February 1997 United announced that for the first time it would enter the international freighter market by providing services to the Pacific rim where the tiger economies constitute the fastest growing markets in the world. From March, United flies two cargo-adapted DC-10-30F aircraft (with a payload capacity of 68,000kg) between Chicago-Anchorage-Los Angeles and on to Osaka-Taipei-Manila six days a week. By autumn 1997 two more DC-10-30s will extend the service to New York-San Francisco-Tokyo. To handle all this increased movement, United intends to use Anchorage as its hub and open a flight operations office and 24hr support centre here. Up to 100 pilots will be stationed here to fly the big freighters.

Code-Share Partners

Code-sharing is now common practice between airlines around the world as it benefits all parties involved by offering a wider network of routes and scheduling to passengers. Competition between airlines is at such a pitch that every little advantage is crucial in winning passengers loyalty.

In 1996 United Airlines had full code-sharing agreements with: Aeromar, Air Canada, ALM Antillean Airlines, Aloha Airlines Inc, Ansett Australia, Ansett New Zealand, British Midland, Cayman Airways, Emirates Airlines, Gulfstream International Airlines, Lufthansa German Airlines and TransBrasil.

Limited Marketing Agreements are held with: Air Malta, Air Nuigini, Austrian Airlines, Biman Bangladesh, Cyprus Airways, Dragonair, Gulf Air, Iberia, Liat Airlines, Malaysian Airlines, National Airlines, Polynesian Airlines, SAETA, Sempati, Thai Airways International, Transaero, TransAsia, VIASA and USAfrica.

Star Alliance

On 14 May 1997 United Airlines, Air Canada, Lufthansa, SAS and Thai International signed an agreement at Frankfurt to unite to form the 'Star Alliance'. Their intention was to create an integrated worldwide air transport network which would provide the airlines' customers with the most comprehensive network of schedules and destinations,

plus a wide range of other benefits. The Star Alliance logo will appear on the fuselage of all aircraft in the fleet giving the alliance global recognition, although each airline will keep its own distinctive brand name and livery. Other airlines, many of whom already have reciprocal arrangements with the five carriers, intend to join the alliance in the future. For example, Varig Brazilian Airlines, the oldest carrier in Latin America, intends to join the alliance in October 1997, as an extension of the links it already has with a number of the airlines. South African Airways and British Midland are currently believed to be seriously examining the benefits of joining the alliance.

Each of the five airlines is already long established in their own extensive domestic markets, as well as running their own international networks; however, together they can offer customers flights to 578 cities in 106 countries: 'The airline network for earth' as they term it. 1,334 aircraft fly an estimated 174.2 million passengers over 229.3 billion miles, accruing $42.3 billion in revenue. In total 210,849 employees work for the alliance, overseeing 6,233 daily departures.

Star Alliance will extend benefits and privileges so that passengers will have easier access to a wider choice of flights and destinations, simplified ticketing and reservations, more convenient connections and better baggage and ground services. The alliance will also combine cargo and maintenance resources and share bookings and airport facilities. Frequent flyers on Star Alliance flights can accumulate mileage points; these points will contribute towards the passenger's elite-level status. Qualifying passengers will be given reciprocal privileges at 179 Star Alliance airport lounges around the world.

Above: *The Boeing Flight Test Center at Seattle in early 1982: 727s, 737s, an AWACS aircraft and — in the foreground — three 767s, two of which were destined for United. N601UA and N602UA were delivered at the end of March and January 1983 respectively.* Boeing

Aircraft Types

United Airlines Aircraft

Above: *One of the earliest 727-22s delivered to United, N7002U saw service from June 1964 to May 1992 — a respectable 28 years.* Austin J. Brown

Boeing 727-222[1]

First flight	27 June 1967
Wingspan	108ft (32.92m)
Wing area	1,700sq ft (157.9sq m)
Length	153ft 2in (46.69m)
Height	34ft (10.36m)
Seating	3 crew, 147 passengers
Cargo volume	25,000cu ft (
Fuel capacity	10,520 US gal (advanced version)
Weight empty	100,000lb (45,360kg)
Max take-off weight	209,500lb (95,030kg)
Max range max fuel	2,400nm (9,450km)
Max range max payload	2,140nm (3,965km)
Cruising speed	467-515kt (865-953km/h)
Powerplant	Three Pratt & Whitney JT8D-17Rs with thrust of 17,400lb (77.3kN)
Max ceiling	42,000ft (12,810m)

Cont

First delivery to United: N7620U on 3 May 1968
Number bought by United: 89 727-22, 38 727-22C (of which 35 were QCs), 104 727-222
Number in service end 1996: 75 727-222

[1]Boeing type numbers identify the first customer, so Boeing 727-200 series aircraft sold to United are identified as 727-222s; those to, for example, American Airlines are 727-223s.

The Boeing 727 is one of the greats of civil aviation. At one stage the 'world's favourite airliner' before being overtaken by the Boeing 737, this medium-range trijet entered production in 1963 and when production ended on 6 April 1984, 1,831 had been sold. Boeing's second jet airliner — following the trail-blazing Boeing 707 — started life in the mid-1950s. The 707, 720 and DC-8 had cornered the long-distance jet market; what was needed was an economic short-range jet airliner. The concept started in the mid-1950s and ended up as a trijet for discussion with potential customers (particularly the biggest US airlines — American, Braniff, Capital, Eastern, Pan Am , TWA, United). Interestingly the trijet configuration was exactly what the 727's initial competitor, the de Havilland Trident, looked like. The 727 benefitted from commonality of parts with Boeing's other two jet stablemates and also from following Trident salesmen who had already promoted the idea of three engines.

The concept worked. UA and Eastern were launch customers; UA had asked for a short-range jet (around 1,500 miles) with c120 economy seats in a six-abreast cabin. It had to be quiet and able to work out of LaGuardia — notorious for its confined space, short runway and noise restrictions. The 727 was ideal for this. The launch order from UA and Eastern was announced on 5 December 1960, each going for 20 firm orders and 20 options. UA's 20 options were predicated on the completion of the merger with Capital which went through on 1 June 1961. The first 727 — N7001U, which was destined for UA — was rolled out on 27 November 1962 with suitable ceremony. This aircraft would be named

Spirit of St Louis in 1988 and be preserved at Paine Field, Washington, by the Museum of Flight Foundation. The 727 first took to the air on 9 February 1963 and received FAA certification on 20 December 1963. United's first delivery was N7004U which was delivered on 29 October 1963; two more followed in late November. United would take 129 of the early models of the 727 (retrospectively named 727-100s after the -200 stretched version appeared). Of these, 38 would be 22Cs — a passenger-cargo model with increased gross weight to 169,000lb and a cargo door — and 35 of these became -22QCs, modified to allow the quick change from passenger to cargo version by having all seats, galleys, lavatories, etc on palletised sections for easy removal.

With such an adaptable and successful airframe, it was not surprising that the 727 was quickly stretched. The 727-200 was stretched by 20ft — 10ft before and after the wing, allowing an extra eight seat rows. United again was a launch customer, ordering six immediately. There was no immediate improvement in engines which meant a reduced payload despite the extra passengers. The -200 was announced in August 1965; roll-out was on 29 June 1967, first flight on 27 July of the same year and certification was approved on 30 November 1967. The engine uprate followed-on, with thrust improving from 14,000lb to 16,000lb.

The final 727 version was the Advanced -200. Designed around an improved thrust P&W JT8D-17 engine, which allowed an increase in maximum take-off weight from 169,000lb to 191,000lb, this enabled additional fuel tanks to be added, improving the range. The Advanced -200 also boasted improved passenger accommodation and noise reduction. Announced in December 1970, it first flew on 29 February 1972. The final JT8D-17R engine with thrust improved to 17,400lb was available from 1976. United would take 104 -222 versions, the first of which was N7620U, delivered on 18 April 1968. The last -222 to reach United was N7467U on 2 July 1980.

The 75 727s left in United service are all Advanced -200s delivered between October 1977 and July 1980. They are used by United on medium-range routes like San Jose to Chicago O'Hare, a 1,829-mile journey taking about 4hr, or Eugene, Oregon, to Denver, Colorado — a 989-mile journey of just over 2hr. Typically the seating layout is 12 first and 135 economy class.

Right: *Typical 727-200 seating arrangement.*

Below: *727-222 N7258U was delivered to United in March 1978 and is still in service. It is seen here two months after delivery over Los Angeles.* J. Wegg

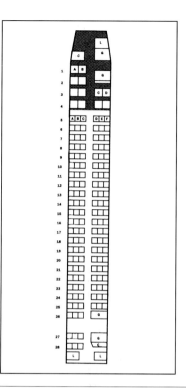

Above: Acquired from Frontier in 1985, 737-291 N7351F was re-registered N994UA in 1986 and is still flying. Note the extended engine nacelles of the 'Advanced' 737-200. Andrew March

Above: 737-322 N389UA was delivered in 1990. Note new livery and the differently shaped engine nacelles in contrast to the picture above. These are high bypass CFM turbofans with flat-bottomed nacelles. Brian S. Strickland

Boeing 737

	737-222[1]	737-322	737-522
First flight	8 August 1967	22 October 1986	5 November 1990
Wingspan	93ft (28.35m)	94ft 9in (28.88m)	94ft 9in (28.88m)
Wing area	1,135sq ft (105.4sq m)	1,135sq ft (105.4sq m)	1,135sq ft (105.4sq m)
Length	100ft 2in (30.53m)	109ft 7in (33.40m)	101ft 9in (31m)
Height	37ft (11.28m)	36ft 6in (11.13m)	36ft 6in (11.13m)
Seating	2 crew, 109 passengers	2 crew, 126 passengers	2 crew, 108 passengers
Cargo volume	875cu ft (24cu m)	1,068cu ft (30cu m)	822cu ft (23cu m)
Fuel capacity	5,160 US gal		
Weight empty	60,600lb (27,448kg)	70,320lb (31,895kg)	68,240lb (30,960kg)
Max take-off weight	115,500lb (52,390kg)	124,500lb (56,472kg)	115,500lb (52,390kg)
Range	1,900-2,300nm (3,519-4,260km)	1,815-2,685nm (3,362-4,973km)	2,420nm (4,485km)
Cruising speed	430-500kt (796-927km/h)	429-491kt (794-908km/h)	430-492kt (795-912kt)
Powerplant	Two Pratt & Whitney JT8D9A 14,500lb (64.5kN) turbofans	Two CFM International CFM56-3B-1s (20,000lb/ 88.97kN) turbofans	Two CFM International CFM56-3B-1 (18,500lb/ 82.3kN) turbofans
Service ceiling	35,000ft (10,675m)	35,000ft (10,675m)	
First delivery to United	29 December 1967	12 November 1986	16 November 1990
Number bought new by United[2]	76[3]	101[5]	57[6]
No in service end 1996	42[4]	101	57

[1]737-200 Advanced.

[2]United still has options on 135 737s.

[3]Delivered 2 in 1967, 41 in 1968 and 33 in 1969.

[4]Includes 24 second-hand Advanced -200s bought from Frontier in June and July 1985 and identified as 737-291s.

[5]Delivered 3 in 1987, 12 in 1987, 34 in 1988, 26 in 1989 and 26 in 1990.

[6]Delivered 4 in 1990, 17 in 1991, 27 in 1992 and 9 in 1993.

The 737 family is the most widely bought jet aircraft; over 3,000 of all types have been sold since the delivery of the first to Lufthansa on 12 December 1967, some eight months after its first flight on 9 April 1967. Designed as a short-range airliner to complement the 727, 720, 707 range, the 737's initial -100 series sold only 30 examples, to four customers, because it had already been overtaken by the -200 series. Developed for airlines requiring greater capacity on short trunk routes, the -200 was a stretch by 6ft, with improved gross weight and fuel capacity.

The 737 first flew on 8 August 1967 and entered service at the same time as the original -100 series, both receiving FAA certification in December 1967. United was the launch customer, receiving N9002U only two days after Lufthansa received its first -100. The type went into service with United, after extensive crew training, on 29 April 1968, by which time United had six of its first order for 40. From early in the programme (May 1971) the -200 was improved, the -200 Advanced appearing with better range, extended engine nacelles housing improved thrust reversers, and increased take-off weight. Kits were made available by Boeing to upgrade earlier-produced -200s.

In the end United acquired more than 70 -200s, buying a number from Frontier in 1985. This was a small part of the 1,114 -200s built, the last of which was delivered in August 1988. By that time the family had moved on: the 737-300 had been announced in March 1981, flying first in February 1984; deliveries began in November 1984, with United taking the first of over 100 737-300s in November 1986. CFM International CFM56 turbofans were substituted for the earlier P&W JT8s, allowing noise reduction to Stage III requirements and improved fuel economy.

The -300 was also stretched by 8ft 8in (2.64m) with a 3ft 8in (1.12m) extension ahead of and one of 5ft (1.53m)

aft of the wing. The -300 benefitted from 757/767 system improvements while retaining much commonality with the -200.

The 737-300 has proved the most successful of the family, followed closely in numbers by the stretched (by 10ft/3.05m) -400 which first flew in February 1988. United did not buy any of this longer-range version, many of which were bought by airlines as 727 replacements. It did buy the -500 series, launched in 1987. At 101ft 9in (31m) in length the 737-500 is currently Boeing's smallest airliner. Its improved fuel economy (thanks once again to the CFM56s) and extensive commonality with the 737-300 and -400 make it a popular choice with airlines requiring short-range high-capacity capability.

With United the 737 covers short-range routes — such as Richmond, Virginia-Chicago O'Hare, a 2hr flight of 642 miles or Denver-Phoenix, 589 miles covered in 1hr 45min — but also takes on longer flights such as Anchorage-Seattle — 1,448 miles covered in 3hr 18min. The seating configurations for all types include 8 first class places; the number of economy seats varies with type — there are 101 economy class seats in the -200, 118 in the -300 and 100 in the -500.

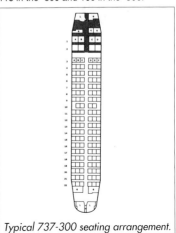

Typical 737-300 seating arrangement.

Above: *747-422 N189UA was delivered in March 1993. It is seen here at Kai Tak.*

Austin J. Brown

Above: *747SP-21 N143UA at Heathrow in March 1994. Originally delivered to Pan Am in 1976, it was bought by United in 1986 and withdrawn from service in 1989.* Austin J. Brown

Boeing 747

	747-122	747-222B	747-422	747SP21
First flight	6 April 1970	1 March 1987	25 May 1989	4 July 1975
Wingspan	195ft 8in (59.64m)	195ft 8in (59.64m)	211ft (64.31m)	195ft 8in (59.64m)
Wing area	5,500sq ft (511sq m)	5,500sq ft (511sq m)	5,650sq ft (525sq m)	5,500sq ft (511sq m)
Length	231ft 10in (70.7m)	231ft 10in (70.7m)	231ft 10in (70.7m)	184ft 9in (56.31m)
Height	63ft 5in (19.3m)	63ft 5in (19.3m)	63ft 5in (19.3m)	65ft 5in (19.94m)
Seating	3 crew, 393-450 pass	3 crew, 264-369 pass	2 crew, 301-418 pass	3 crew, 316 pass
Cargo volume	3,843cu ft (108cu m)	5,763cu ft (163cu m)	5,643cu ft (159cu m)	
Fuel capacity				
Weight empty	358,000lb (162,386kg)	374,400lb (169,960kg)	399,000lb (180,985kg)	325,000lb (147,720kg)
Max take-off weight	750,000lb (340,195kg)	833,000lb (377,840kg)	800,000-870,000lb (362,875-394,625kg)	700,000lb (317,515kg)
Range	4,900nm (9,050km) (with 366 pass)	6,900nm (12,778km) (with 366 pass)	7,340nm (13,600km) (with 400 pass)	5,855nm (10,840km) (with 331 pass)
Cruising speed	490kt (907km/h)	507kt	507kt	540kt (1,000km/h)
Powerplant	Four P&W JT9D-3 43,000lb (191.26kN) thrust turbofans (first models; thereafter -7As and -7Fs of 46,950-48,000lb (208.9-213.5kN)	Four P&W JT9D-7R4G2 54,750lb (243.5kN) thrust turbofans	Four P&W PW4056 56,750lb (252.39kN) thrust turbofans	Four P&W JT9D-7AW 48,750lb (218.4kN) thrust turbofans
Service ceiling	45,000ft (13,725m)	45,000ft (13,725m)	45,000ft (13,725m)	45,000ft (13,725m)
First delivery to United	30 June 1970	19 March 1987	30 June 1989	
Number bought new by United	18[1]	2[2]	22[3]	0
Number in service end 1996	18[4]	9[5]	24[6]	3[7]

[1]Delivered: 9 in 1970, 3 in 1971, 2 in 1972 and 4 in 1973.
[2]Both delivered in 1987.
[3]Delivered: 3 in 1989, 5 in 1990, 4 in 1991, 6 in 1992, 4 in 1993.
[4]Includes 5 second-hand -123s originally delivered to American Airlines and bought by United between September 1987 and January 1988.
[5]Includes 7 second-hand -238Bs delivered originally to Qantas between May 1975 and October 1978 and bought or leased by United between March 1991 and October 1992.
[6]Includes 2 -451s bought from Boeing in mid-1994 from an original Northwest Airlines order which wasn't taken up. United has a further 15 -422s on order and options on a total of 40.
[7]United's 3 SP21s are all second-hand aircraft originally delivered to Pan Am, May 1977-June 1978. United acquired them in February 1986.

The 747 saw a quantum jump in civil aviation. It was the first of a new generation of wide-bodied airliners changing the face of long-haul air travel.

Crucial to its appearance were three main factors: first, the realisation that such an aircraft was likely to be commercially viable and that its greater capacity could be filled — this was shown in 1964 when reduced-fare policies saw passenger traffic increase by 30%; second, the technology existed to build such an aircraft — Boeing's work on the USAF's CX-HLS (the Cargo Experimental-Heavy Lift System project won by Lockheed with the C-5 Galaxy) convinced the company it could; finally, with all aircraft manufacturers of the time expecting supersonic transport to take over inside 10 years, Boeing pragmatically went for a design that could accommodate a substantial cargo either as a separate cargo aircraft, or as a combination of passengers and cargo. The aircraft was launched in mid-1966, Pan Am being the launch customer with an order for 25 aircraft at the then huge price of $20 million each. Today Boeing's price for a new 747-400 is $156-$174 million!

The first 747, N7470, flew on 9 February 1969, the type receiving certification on 30 December of the same year. The 747 entered service with Pan Am in January 1970, the first of 176 -100s and -100Bs. It changed the whole concept of air travel with 10-abreast seating, substantial freight capacity and economy of use. United's first 747, N4703U, called *William M. Allen*, was delivered in June 1970, the first of nine delivered in the year. After an improved -100B announced late in autumn 1977 and bought by only three customers, the major -100 variation was the 747SP — Special Performance — designed to reduce weight and so reduce costs. Shortened by 47ft 1in (14.35m), with a bigger tailplane, the SPs set incredible long-distance records (one flew to Cape Town from the factory nonstop, a then record distance of 8,940nm/16,560km). Pan Am was again the launch customer and United bought none new, but when the company bought Pan Am's transpacific routes in 1986, it bought Pan Am's 10 SP21s and also an SP27 (N529PA *Clipper America* which became N150UA) that Pan Am had acquired from Braniff. Today United has disposed of most of its SPs, with the remaining three in store.

The next model to be bought by United was the -200B which first flew on 11 October 1970. Substantially heavier, with improved engines and therefore maximum take-off weight, the -200B (there were no -200As) became the standard build until the -400 came along. (In between there were a variety of 747 variants — many involving cargo/passenger combinations — and the 747-300, with a stretched upper deck.) The -400 series provided a major revamp of the 747 and set the type up for delivery into the next millennium. It operates at much higher gross weights with more powerful engines than the -200, allowing greater increases in both range and payload, and has drag reducing 6ft-high wingtip winglets, a completely redesigned EFIS flightdeck, borrowing from that of the 757 and 767, and substantial weight savings through the use of new alloys. It first flew in 1988, United taking its first in June 1989.

In United service the 747s are used primarily for long-haul flights — such as Los Angeles-Hong Kong (a 7,247-mile flight negotiated in 14hr 35min), Los Angeles-Sydney (7,487 miles), Chicago O'Hare-Hong Kong (7,787 miles) or Chicago-Honolulu (4,283 miles). Seating arrangements vary, with the timetable showing two or three class configurations for 747-100s — 18 first, 70 business and 305 economy or 42 first and 408 economy; the -200s can be configured 35-105-124 or 18-79-272; the -400s either 36-123-142 or 18-80-320.

Above: *747-122 N4732U at London Heathrow in April 1991. This aircraft has been in service with United since March 1973.* Austin J. Brown

Above: *The Boeing 757, after a sluggish start, is picking up customers as business expands on shorter routes rendering 727s and 737s too small. On top of this, the ETOPS rating has allowed more flexibility. 757-222ER N548UA has been with United since 1992. It is seen here in 1993 at Washington.* Peter R. March

Below: *N583UA, another 757-222, seen in new livery.* Austin J. Brown

Boeing 757

	757-222
First flight	19 February 1982
Wingspan	124ft 10in (38.05m)
Wing area	1,994sq ft (185.25sq m)
Length	155ft 3in (47.32m)
Height	44ft 6in (13.56m)
Seating	2 crew, 188 passengers
Cargo volume	1,698cu ft (48cu m)
Fuel capacity	75,500lb (34,277kg)
Weight empty	129,100lb (58,611kg)
Max take-off weight	240,000lb (108,960kg)
Range	3,700nm (6,857km)
Cruising speed	460kt (850km/h)
Powerplant	2 P&W PW2037 38,200lb (170kN) thrust turbofans
Service ceiling	42,000ft (12,810m)
First delivery to United	24 August 1989
Number bought by United	92[1]
Number in service end 1996	92

[1]Deliveries: 5 in 1989, 19 in 1990, 23 in 1991, 27 in 1992, 14 in 1993 plus 4 since.

With the 727 getting long in the tooth, Boeing had been looking for a suitable replacement. The first thought was simply to stretch the reliable and best-selling trijet 727 itself. Indeed, this is what was shown in 1974 and at the Paris Air Show in 1975. United had shown interest in this 727-300B, a stretch that would increase passenger numbers to 189 and the improved engines would take the range out to 2,300 miles (3,700km), but no airline would put in a confirmed order because of the need for quieter and more fuel-efficient engines — a particular issue in the oil crisis of the 1970s.

Boeing therefore changed tack and, after a variety of design changes, in February 1978 it reached a formula, now christened 757, that proved successful enough to gain orders. It used the 727's fuselage cross-section, a new flightdeck, a modified empennage and a totally new wing. It was designed to carry 150-170 passengers, and would have a pair of fuel-efficient, quiet turbofans. This 757 was launched in March 1979; British Airways and Eastern were launch customers. To save costs there was commonality of systems with the 767, especially in the flightdeck and avionics equipment — so much so that pilots could be cleared to fly both 757 and 767 without conversion. The 757 was produced in parallel with the 767 — the latter actually the first to fly despite the numerical sequence.

The 757 took to the air on 19 February 1982 and received certification on 17 December 1982 (FAA) and in January 1983 (CAA). Entering service in January 1983 with Eastern, the early 757-200s were the first Boeing aircraft launched with non-American powerplants, being powered by Rolls-Royce RB211-535Cs (this was no coincidence considering BA was one of the launch customers). First flight of a US (Pratt & Whitney)-engined version was on 14 March 1984. The 757-200 was one of the first aircraft to have electronic displays, with many routine tasks automated. It quickly established itself on the world market and has gone through little developmental change since. In 1985 the 757-200ER was certified for ETOPS with Rolls-Royce engines, followed by Pratt & Whitney-powered versions in 1990. (See 767 section for explanation of the acronym ETOPS, now known as EROPS.)

United took some time to come into the 757 market, but by 1988 decided to replace 29 DC-8s with 757s. Apart from the improved specification and quieter engines,

the commonality with the rest of its Boeing fleet was a major advantage. United placed its 30 firm/30 option order for Pratt & Whitney-engined 757s in May 1988, with deliveries scheduled to take place from 1989 to 1991. In April 1989 the initial order was doubled to 60 firm/60 options; three months later the first United aircraft, N501UA, flew on 26 July and was delivered a month later. The timetable shows a 24 first and 164 economy class configuration for United's 757s, with flights to a variety of continental United States and overseas locations such as Kahului, Hawaii-San Francisco (2,338 miles, 4hr 42min), Washington Dulles-Los Angeles (2,288 miles, 4hr 43min), San Francisco-Newark, New Jersey (2,565 miles, 5hr 25min).

Boeing 767

	767-222	767-222ER	767-322ER
First flight	26 September 1981	6 March 1984	19 December 1986
Wingspan	156ft 1in (47.57m)	156ft 1in (47.57m)	156ft 4in/47.64m
Wing area	3,050sq ft (283.2sq m)	3,050sq ft (283.2sq m)	3,050sq ft/283.2sq m
Length	159ft 2in (48.51m)	159ft 2in (48.51m)	180ft 3in/54.94m
Height	52ft (15.85m)	52ft (15.85m)	52ft/15.85m
Seating	2/3 crew, +172	2/3 crew, +166	2crew,+202
Cargo volume	3,070cu ft (86cu m)	3,070cu ft (87cu m)	4,030cu ft/114.1cu m
Fuel capacity	112,309lb (50,988kg)	137,527lb (62,437kg)	161,738lb/73,429kg
Weight empty	164,800lb (74,752kg)	168,600lb (76,476kg)	205,600lb/93,342kg
Max T/o weight	300,000lb (136,078kg)	387,000lb (175,540kg)	400,000lb/181,600kg
Range	3,160nm (5,855km)	6,805nm (12,611km)	5,760nm/10,674km
Cruising speed	461kt (854km/h)	493kt (914km/h)	486kt/900km/h
Powerplant	2 Pratt & Whitney JT9D-7R4Ds 48,000lb (213.5kN) thrust turbofans	2 Pratt & Whitney PW4056 56,750lb (252.4kN) thrust turbofans	2 Pratt & Whitney PW4060 60,000lb (266.87kN) thrust turbofans
Service ceiling	40,000ft (12,192m)	40,000ft (12,192m)	42,000ft (12,810m)
First delivery to United	19 August 1982	Note [1]	18 April 1991
Number bought by United	11	8	23
Number in service end 1996	11[2]	8[2]	23[2]

[1]Deliveries: 7 in 1982, 1 in 1983, 11 in 1983; then -322ER 5 in 1991, 10 in 1992, 8 in 1993.
[2]767-222s uprated to ER standard.

Above: *767-222ER N607UA* City of Denver *was one of the earliest 767s to be delivered to United – in September 1982.* Austin J. Brown

Above: *767-322ER N663UA was delivered in August 1993. Seen here at London Heathrow in April 1997.* Philip J. Birtles

The 767 project first saw light of day when Boeing released drawings of a 200-passenger, four-engined (two underwing, two on rear fuselage) aircraft in August 1971. As is always the case with a new jet aircraft, development time is considerable and the upturn of 737 sales meant that Boeing was in no hurry to produce an in-house competitor. It was, therefore, only in February 1978 that Boeing announced its future 757, 767 and 777 projects.

The 767-100 was an all-new wide-bodied aircraft which had been designed to fit an American Airlines requirement to carry 175 passengers in a seven-abreast configuration over a range of 2,000nm; the 767-200 had extra seating and was based on a United requirement for 190 passengers to be carried. It was the latter that, following more design changes, became the final 767 with United as launch customer on 14 July 1978 with an order for 30 planned for mid-1982 entry into service. In November 1978 options were placed on a further 37 aircraft, nine of these becoming firm in September 1980. The unit price of a 767 at that time was $25 million — which shows how inflation hit prices; today's costing for a 767-200 is $77-87 million.

Just as the battle between the Airbus A310 and the 767 had been intensely competitive, so was the battle between Pratt & Whitney and General Electric for the engine contract. United plumped for P&W JT9Ds — derated and modified versions of the 747's engines. The first 767 flew on 26 September 1981 and the type entered service the next year. But bad news for Boeing was just around the corner. The recession of the 1980s began to bite and in June 1982 United was forced to cancel 20 of the 39 firm orders because of the failure of the US economy. In fact, as things improved, United would buy more than 40 767s of all variants.

The 767 was intended for medium-range routes of up to 3,000nm and could carry a maximum of 290 passengers, though more typically 216 passengers are carried in two classes. United's 767-200s in domestic service were originally configured to take a mixture of six-abreast (24 first class) and seven abreast (173 economy class), but today's timetable has a three-class configuration of 10 first, 33 business and 125 economy class.

The certification of the P&W-engined version was achieved on 30 July 1982 and on 19 August United's first 767 was delivered, Boeing president Malcolm T. Stamper handing over the keys to United's chairman Richard J. Ferris during a ceremony at the Everett plant. The aircraft was the ninth off the line and was flown to San Francisco. Commercial services were inaugurated on 9 August with a flight from Chicago to Denver. Quickly 767s began to take over such services as those flown by DC-10s on routes to San Francisco, New York LaGuardia and Boston. Four more 767s were delivered to UA by the end of October, increasing to eight by early 1983. By October 1982 services covered Portland, Seattle, Detroit and Newark. The deliveries on hold were rescheduled for five a year from 1985 to 1988, although in reality, following delivery of the 19th aircraft in April 1983, it would not be until 1991 that United took possession of another 767.

The longer-range -200ER version — with an extra wing-section fuel tank— first flew on 6 March 1984, entering service in May of that year. The next 767 development saw Boeing produce the stretched 767-300 which flew first on 30 January 1986. The 21ft 1in (6.42m) stretch saw two sections added to the fuselage in front of and behind the wing. At the end of 1986 the extended range version of the 767-300 flew for the first time. American was launch customer for this version, ordering 15. United ordered 16 in May 1989 with options for a further 16, all to be P&W-engined.

The economic use of reliable, extended range twin-jets over transoceanic — especially transatlantic — routes required highly significant change to ETOPS (Extended range Twin-jet Operations) established by US FAA 1953 diktat, which said that twin-engined aircraft must always be within an hour of an airfield at zero wind speed and normal cruising speed — this usually worked out to be 400nm (841km).

While it was possible — as TWA showed by inaugurating the first 767 nonstop transcontinental flights — to fly these distances, the 60min rule reduced the economic use of twin-jets over the Atlantic. Fuel costs and the substantial improvement in engine reliability since the original 1953 pronouncement led to an extension of the length of time twin-engined aircraft can operate over oceans to 120min, assuming the engine/aircraft

combination gets certified. (The acronym ETOPS became EROPS — Extended Range Operations — in 1989.)

The 767s have proved to be more than capable of long-distance, over-water flying as is shown by their timetabled services, such as those to and from London Heathrow: a flight to JFK of 3,452 miles is timetabled to be accomplished in 7hr 55min. Other examples of 767 services are: Delhi-London Heathrow (4,190 miles in 10hr), JFK-Los Angeles (2,475 miles, 5hr 46min), Boston-San Francisco (2,704 miles, 6hr 18min). Seating configurations of the 767-222 on non-domestic services are 10 first, 32 second and 126 economy class; the stretched 767-322 seating 10-38-158.

Boeing 777-200

First flight	14 June 1994
Wingspan	199ft 11in (60.9m)
Wing area	4,605sq ft (427.8m)
Length	209ft 1in (63.72m)
Height	60ft 6in (18.44m)
Seating	2 crew, 292 passengers
Cargo volume	5,720cu ft (162cu m)
Fuel capacity	31,600 US gal
Max take-off weight	580,000lb (263,085kg)
Range	7,705nm (12,415km)
Cruising speed	Mach 0.83
Powerplant	2 Pratt & Whitney PW4074 74,000lb (332kN) thrust turbofans
Service ceiling	43,000ft (13,136m)

First delivery to United May 1995
Number bought by United 16 to date; orders for 12 for 1997, 4 for 1998 and 2 for 1999.
Number in service end 1996 16

The 777 is a state-of-the-art, fully fly-by-wire advanced technology high capacity wide-bodied aircraft, and one with which United has been intimately involved from the start. Indeed, the airline acted as the leader and co-ordinator of eight airlines who discussed the concept together to

achieve performance in tune with their requirements. With this careful groundwork, the 777 has evolved into a remarkable new aircraft full of all the latest technology and one which will take Boeing into the 21st century. The 777 programme was launched in October 1990, with deliveries to launch

Above: *United has ordered 34 777's with an option for 34 more reflecting a total investment of $4 billion. This is 777-222 N770UA at London Heathrow, January 1997.* Austin J. Brown

Above: *Another view of N770UA at London Heathrow, January 1997.* Austin J. Brown

customer United in 1995. United's initial order was for 34, with options on a further 34. Combined with a simultaneous order for 60 Boeing 747-400s, it was the largest deal in aviation history, worth $22 billion. The 777 comes in two forms — 'A' and 'B' — where 'A' is the domestic US version and 'B' is the longer-range version. Interestingly, the 747 prototype, N7470, which had been donated to the Seattle Museum of Flight was leased back to Boeing as a 777 engine testbed. The 777 entered service with United on 17 May 1995. From January 1997, following the announcement of the GE90's clearance for extended range, United flew 777s from Chicago to London Heathrow. United Airlines introduced the new, long-range 777B to Los Angeles with a daily service to London Heathrow beginning on June 5. The 777 replaced the smaller 767 on the route. Configured for 292-seat, three-class accommodation as the existing 777As, the higher thrust engines and other modifications give the 777B additional range and payload capability.

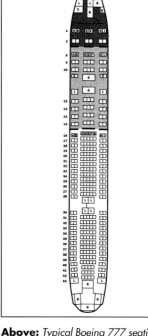

Below: *United Airlines DC10-10 at Denver, 1989.* Austin J. Brown

Above: *Typical Boeing 777 seating arrangement.*

McDonnell Douglas DC-10

	DC-10-10	DC-10-30
First flight	29 August 1970	21 June 1972
Wingspan	155ft 4in (47.34m)	165ft 4in (50.39m)
Wing area	3,550sq ft (329.8sq m)	3,647sq ft (338.8sq m)
Length	182ft 3in (55.3m)	180ft 8in (55.06m)
Height	58ft 1in (17.7m)	58ft 1in (17.7m)
Seating	3 crew, 237-290 passengers	3 crew, 273 passengers
Cargo volume	3,180cu ft (89cu m)	3,655cu ft (103.5cu m)
Fuel capacity	145,200lb (65,921kg)	245,566lb (111,420kg)
Weight empty	248,100lb (112,637kg)	267,197lb (121,198kg)
Max take-off weight	430,000lb (195,200kg)	580,000lb (263,085kg)
Max range max fuel	3,800nm (7,040km)	6,505nm (12,055km)
Max range max payload	2,000nm (3,700km)	4,005nm (7,415km)
Cruising speed	464kt (860km/h)	490kt (908km/h)
Powerplant	3 x General Electric (GE) CF6-6D 40,000lb (178kN) or D1 41,000lb (182.4kN) thrust turbofans	3 x GE CF6-50C 51,000lb (226.9kN) thrust turbofans
Service ceiling	42,000ft (12,810m)	42,000ft (12,810m)
First delivery to United	29 July 1971	Second-hand from 1984
Number bought by United	47[1]	8[2]
Number in service end 1996	44[3]	8[4]

[1] 2 in 1971, 16 in 1972, 5 in 1973, 7 in 1974, 7 in 1975, 1 in 1979, 4 in 1980, 4 in 1981, 1 in 1982

[2] Includes 4 DC-10-30CFs. All bought second-hand, the -30s 3 in 1984, 1 in 1985, the -30CFs in 1986.

[3] Includes 17 stored; 36 due for FedEx.

[4] Includes 4 DC-10-30CFs.

The DC-10 was born out of the US Air Force's CX-HLS heavy-lift cargo requirement, which led to competitive studies from Boeing (whose submission helped considerably the development of the 747), Lockheed (the eventual winner with the C-5 Galaxy) and Douglas. In the aftermath of the loss of this order there was an attempt to produce a civil version — a 650-seat, double-deck, wide-bodied aircraft which was just too big for the time.

At this juncture American Airlines circulated to the same big three companies — Boeing, Lockheed and Douglas — a specification for the size of aircraft it required to increase its passenger-carrying abilities without increasing air movements.

American proposed an aircraft that should be able to carry 250 passengers in wide-bodied comfort over ranges of 1,000-2,000 miles depending on the length of the runways used. Merger with McDonnell on 28 April 1967 eased Douglas's financial problems and the DC-10 became the first McDonnell Douglas aircraft and the last to carry the famous 'DC' branding. McDonnell Douglas's capital, and a new project manager, saw the response to American's proposal refined down to its final form — a trijet, the third engine being necessary to give the additional power needed for the aircraft to use shorter runways.

While American signed the first order for the DC-10, the aircraft could not have gone

Above: *DC-10-10 N1809U at Los Angeles in 1993. After nearly 20 years service, in 1993 it was withdrawn and stored. It was then sold to FedEx.* Leo Marriott

ahead without the order from United who chose it over the TriStar. Without doubt, loss of the DC-10 would have been a grievous, possibly terminal blow for McDonnell Douglas, and United felt that this would be bad for competition.

The first DC-10s were handed over to American and United (who had ordered 60 — 30 firm and 30 on option) in a joint ceremony at Long Beach on 29 July 1971 and the type entered United service on 14 August when N1802U took charge of a San Francisco-Washington flight. The DC-10 replaced United's DC-8-50s and -60s: it proved perfect for United's transcontinental routes. The DC-10-30, an intercontinental version with uprated engines, was rolled out on 1 June 1972 and first flight took place three weeks later. It entered commercial service with Swissair on 15 December 1972.

The -10-30, with an intercontinental range of almost 5,900 miles, found its slot on routes too small for the Boeing 747. Using the -10s on its vast array of domestic routes, the United fleet reached 41 on delivery of -10CF N1848U on 20 September 1982. Between 31 August and 21 September 1984 three ex-Laker -30s were acquired from McDonnell Douglas, with another added from Pan Am and four -30CFs from World Airlines over the next two years. After 20 years' service,

withdrawal of early -10s started in 1993, many of them being stored for FedEx for whom 36 of United's 44 -10s are destined.

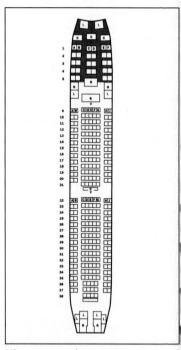

Above: *Typical DC-10-10 seating arrangement.*

Above: *United took delivery of the first of its Airbus A319s — N802UA — at Toulouse on 30 June 1997. It was the first of 28 A319s on order.* Airbus Industrie

Airbus A320-232

First flight	22 February 1987
Wingspan	111ft 10in (34.1m)
Wing area	1,320sq ft (123m)
Length	123ft 3in (37.57m)
Height	38ft 9in (11.8m)
Seating	2 crew, 144 passengers
Cargo volume	1,270cu ft (36cu m)
Max take-off weight	580,000lb (263,085kg)
Range	7,705nm (12,415km)
Cruising speed	Mach 0.83
Powerplant	2 Pratt & Whitney Type PW4073 with total thrust of 73,000lb (327kN)

First delivery to United 24 November 1993

Number bought by United 36 to date; orders for 6 for 1997, 8 for 1998.

Number in service end 1996 36 (deliveries — 5 in 1993, 16 in 1994, 10 in 1995, and 5 in 1996)

A320

The Airbus A320 was the second design by the Airbus consortium following in the successful footsteps of the A310. A short/medium-range airliner powered by twin turbofans, it attracted considerable interest from world airlines, with over 400 orders before its first flight. United ordered 50 and received its first A320-232 in November 1993. Since then it has taken on a range of services — such as Los Angeles-Chicago (1,744 miles/2,806km in 3hr 50min), Boston-Chicago (869 miles/1,430km 2hr 27min) Los Angeles-Newark (2,454 miles/3,950km in 5hr 18min) and Los Angeles-Boston (2,611 miles/4,200km in 5hr 23min). The A320 is known for its computerised fly-by-wire technology (it was the first airliner to be so equipped); it has a highly advanced cockpit with EFIs displays and sidestick controls. The multi-functional displays are in colour, it boasts a unique Centralised Aircraft Monitor System and only 13 main panel instruments. It was launched in 1984 with first deliveries of the A320-100 version (to Air France) in 1988. The first -200 operator was Ansett. Typical seat configuration with United is 12 First Class and 132 Economy.

A319

The Airbus A319 was launched at the 1993 Farnborough Air Show. A short-range twin turbofan-engined airliner, it is the smallest of the successful Airbus family and was given a big boost by United's order. A de-stretched version of the A320, United Airlines launched its first A319 service on 8 July 1997, some eight days after accepting its first aircraft from Airbus Industrie in Toulouse. United launched services with the first two of 28 A319s ordered. The initial schedule called for flights linking Chicago with Boston, Los Angeles, Santa Ana (Orange County), and Washington National. The A319s were ferried over via Toronto. The seat configuration for United's A319s is eight seats in First Class and 118 in Economy for a total of 126.

Airbus A319

First flight	25 April 1995
Wingspan	111ft 10in (34.1m)
Wing area	1,320sq ft (123m)
Length	111ft (33.83m)
Height	38ft 7in (11.8m)
Seating	2 crew, 126 passengers
Max payload	37,200lb(16,890kg)
Max take-off weight	149,900lb (68,055kg)
Range	3,000nm (5,560km)
Cruising speed	Mach 0.83
Powerplant	2 IAE V2500 engines
First delivery to United	30 June 1997
Number bought by United	2 to date; orders for 26 1997-8.

Below: *Airbus A320-232 N408UA* Peter C. Bond Customer *was delivered in March 1994.* Airbus Industrie

Above: *Airbus A320-232 N408UA was delivered in 1994.*
Airbus Industrie via Peter R. March

United Express Aircraft

BAe ATP

First flight	6 August 1986
Wingspan	100ft 6in (30.63m)
Length	85ft 4in (26.01m)
Height	24ft 11in (7.59m)
Seating	2 crew, 64 passengers
Range	800nm (1,480km)
Cruising speed	236kt max (437km/h)
Powerplant	2 x Pratt & Whitney Canada 2,653shp (1,978kW) PW126A turboprops driving six-bladed props
Used by	United Feeder Service

Number in fleet end 1996 9

This large regional airliner was developed from the HS748 and after sales had ceased at the low level of 65, it was resurrected as the Jetstream 61. Quiet, with good economics, reliability problems in its early years kept sales low, despite its obvious plus points. Example services: Chicago-Akron/Canton, Ohio 344 miles (1hr 45min), South Bend, Indiana-Chicago 84 miles (41min).

BAe 146-100/-200/-300

Data	146-300
First flight	1 May 1987
Wingspan	86ft (26.21m)
Length	101ft 8in (30.99m)
Height	28ft 3in (8.61m)
Seating	2 crew, 100 passengers
Range	1,040nm (1,927km) with max payload
Cruising speed	426kt max (790km/h)
Powerplant	4 x Textron Lycoming ALF 502R-5 6,970lb (31kN) turbofans
Used by	Air Wisconsin

Number in fleet end 1996 -100 — 2; 200 — 8 (including 3 on lease); -300 — 5

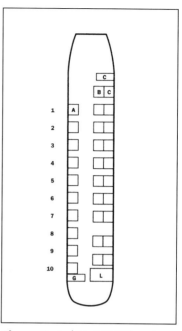

Above: *Typical BAe146-100 seating arrangement.*

A very quiet and versatile series of regional airliners developed from the Hawker Siddeley HS146. The first -100 series (some 15ft 9in/5m shorter than the -300) flew on 3 September 1981. Air Wisconsin was the launch customer for both -200 and -300, which entered service in June 1983 and December 1988 respectively. Seating configurations give 86 passengers at six-abreast (-100), 86 at five-abreast (-200) and 100 at five-abreast (-300).

Example flights: Denver-Milwaukee, 908 miles (2hr 40min), Chicago-Milwaukee, 67 miles (35min).

BAe Jetstream 41/Super 31

Data	41
First flight	25 September 1991
Wingspan	60ft (18.29m)
Length	63ft 2in (19.25m)
Height	18ft 10in (5.37m)
Seating	2 crew, 29 passengers
Range	681nm (1,263km)
Cruising speed	260kt (482km/h)
Powerplant	2 x Garrett 1,500shp (1,119kW) TPE331-14GR turboprops driving five-bladed props
Used by	Atlantic Coast Airlines

Number in fleet end 1996 Jetstream 41 — 28 plus 12 on order; 31 — 30

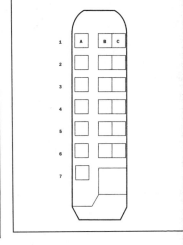

Developed from the Handley Page HP37 which first flew in 1967, the Jetstream family of feederliners is configured to carry 19 passengers (31) or 29 (41) in a three-abreast layout. Example flights: J41 Portland-Washington Dulles, 494 miles (2h 10min), J31 Los Angeles-Orange County, 31 miles (30min).

Beechcraft 1900C-1/D

Data	1900C-1
First flight	3 September 1982
Wingspan	54ft 6in (16.60m)
Length	57ft 10in (17.63m)
Height	14ft 11in (4.54m)
Seating	2 crew, 19 passengers
Range	1,570nm max (2,907km)
Cruising speed	267kt max (495km/h)
Powerplant	2 x Pratt & Whitney Canada 1,100shp (820kW) PT6A-65B turboprops driving four-bladed props
Used by	Great Lakes Airlines, Mountain West Airlines

Number in fleet end 1996 1900C-1 — 25; 1900D — 30 (of which 20 MWA)

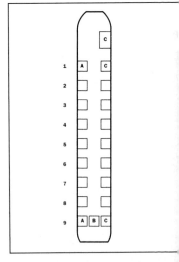

The Beechraft 1900 twin-engined feederliner received FAA certification in November 1983. The C-1 has a 'wet' wing (ie extra fuel tanks carried). The 1900D came in during 1991 and flew first with Mesa, one of the United Express carriers. Example flights: Sioux City-Denver, 466 miles (2hr), Denver-Mattoon, Illinois, 61

Above: *BAe146-100 N246SS seen when part of Aspen Air at Denver in July 1989. Aspen merged with Air Wisconsin in 1991. Air Wisconsin has 12 BAe146s and leases others.* Austin J. Brown

Below: *Beechcraft 1900D N50YV was delivered to Mesa Air in 1993.* Leo Marriott

Embraer EMB-120ER/-120RT Brasilia

Data	EMB-120ER
Wingspan	64ft 11in (19.78m)
Length	65ft 10in (20.07m)
Height	20ft 10in (6.35m)
Seating	2 crew, 30 passengers
Range	810nm (1,500km)
Cruising speed	300kt (555km/h)
Powerplant	2 x Pratt & Whitney Canada 1,800shp (1,340kW) PW18 turboprops driving four-bladed props
Used by	Great Lakes Airlines, Mountain West Airlines, WestAir

Number in fleet end 1996 RT — 25 (GLA 5, MWA 2 [including 1 on lease], W 18), ER — 7 (GLA 5 with 2 on order, MWA 1, W 1)

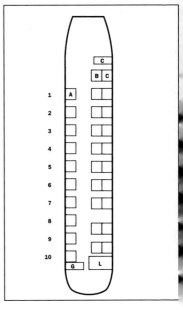

Developed in the late 1970s, the first pre-production flight of this twin-engined STOL airliner was in 1983. The original -100 version was stretched by 11ft 3in (3.43m) to produce the -300. The -200 series, available since 1994, had greater commonality with the -300 and PW123C engines. Seating configurations are four-abreast in both the smaller -200 (37 passengers) and larger -300. Example flights: Denver-Grand Junction, Colorado, 212 miles (1hr 10min), Denver-Junction Hole, Wyoming, 406 miles (1hr 55min).

DHC-8

Data	Dash 8-300
First flight	15 May 1987
Wingspan	90ft (27.43m)
Length	84ft 3in (25.68m)
Height	24ft 7in (7.49m)
Seating	2 crew, 50 passengers
Range	1,250nm (2,315km)
Cruising speed	287kt max (532km/h)
Powerplant	2 x Pratt & Whitney Canada 2,380shp (1,775kW) PW123 Turboprops driving four-bladed props
Used by	Mountain West Airlines

Number in fleet end 1996 10 (-200 — 9, -300 —1)

A pressurised Bandeirante launched in September 1979, the Extended Range version arrived in 1992 and kits were made available to uprate existing aircraft. The -120RT is a reduced take-off weight version. This twin-engined regional airliner entered service in 1985. Example flights: Denver-Bismarck, North Dakota, 516 miles (1hr 55min), San Francisco-Eureka, California, 250 miles (1hr 10min).

Above: N132EM, an EMBRAIR EMB-110 Bandeirante, was leased by United Express's WestAir Commuter Services from 1986-90. Today the EMB-120 Brasilia has replaced it. Austin J. Brown

Below: WestAir Holdings ordered up to 52 Jetstream 31s for delivery through to 1992 for use on United Express services. BAe via Ian Allan Library

Fleet List

Registration	Aircraft Type/Notes		Registration	Aircraft Type/Notes	
N801UA	Airbus A319-130	Delivered 7/97	N	Airbus A319-130	on order 10/97
N802UA	Airbus A319-130	Delivered 7/97	N	Airbus A319-130	on order 11/97
N	Airbus A319-130	on order 8/97	N	Airbus A319-130	on order 12/97
N	Airbus A319-130	on order 9/97			

Registration	Aircraft Type	Notes/Names
N401UA	Airbus A320-232	*Alan Temple Employee*
N402UA	Airbus A320-232	*Telma Aloni Employee*
N403UA	Airbus A320-232	*Hiroko Fujishima Employee*
N404UA	Airbus A320-232	*Maria Karla Gozum Employee*
N405UA	Airbus A320-232	*John P. Macri Sr Customer*
N406UA	Airbus A320-232	*J. Rex Pippin Customer*
N407UA	Airbus A320-232	*Jeff Mandlebaum Customer*
N408UA	Airbus A320-232	*Peter C. Bond Customer*
N409UA	Airbus A320-232	*Bob Young Customer*
N410UA	Airbus A320-232	*C. Nicholas Keating Jr Customer*
N411UA	Airbus A320-232	*Kaz Imal Customer*
N412UA	Airbus A320-232	*Romert Thomas Customer*
N413UA	Airbus A320-232	*Jeff Wild Customer*
N414UA	Airbus A320-232	*Toshi K. Funaki Customer*
N415UA	Airbus A320-232	*Ronald A. Schy*
N416UA	Airbus A320-232	*Timothy L. Devine Customer*
N417UA	Airbus A320-232	*Rickey Wilson Customer*
N418UA	Airbus A320-232	*Scott Setrakian Customer*
N419UA	Airbus A320-232	*M. J. Suhanovsky Customer*
N420UA	Airbus A320-232	*Charles A. Kelley Customer*
N421UA	Airbus A320-232	*Peter A. Dare Customer*
N422UA	Airbus A320-232	*Yale R. Brown Customer*
N423UA	Airbus A320-232	*Ron Maehl Customer*
N424UA	Airbus A320-232	*Albert G. Brantley Customer*
N425UA	Airbus A320-232	*Howard J. Morgan Customer*
N426UA	Airbus A320-232	*William Yeack Customer*
N427UA	Airbus A320-232	*Dee Groberg Customer*
N428UA	Airbus A320-232	*Robert J. Viscio Customer*
N429UA	Airbus A320-232	
N430UA	Airbus A320-232	
N431UA	Airbus A320-232	
N432UA	Airbus A320-232	
N433UA	Airbus A320-232	
N434UA	Airbus A320-232	
N435UA	Airbus A320-232	
N436UA	Airbus A320-232	
N437UA	Airbus A320-232	on order 6/97

Above: *A320 N401UA was the first Airbus to be delivered to United in November 1993. By June 1997, United's Airbus fleet had swelled to 80 in service or on order.* Airbus via Peter R. March

Below: *Airbus A319 in United colours.* Airbus

Registration	Aircraft Type	Notes/Names
N438UA	Airbus A320-232	on order 6/97
N439UA	Airbus A320-232	on order 7/97
N	Airbus A320-232	on order 8/97
N	Airbus A320-232	on order 10/97
N	Airbus A320-232	on order 10/97

Above: *A320 N405UA leaving Washington National.* Philip J. Birtles

Below: *The Airbus A319s are delivered to United staging through Toronto. Here, on 1 July 1997, N801UA is at Terminal 3 having arrived some 30 minutes after N802UA.* Michael L. Baker

Above: *A320 in United colours on test flight.* United Airlines

Registration/Aircraft Type		Registration/Aircraft Type		Registration/Aircraft Type	
N7251U	Boeing 727-222	N7276U	Boeing 727-222	N7444U	Boeing 727-222
	stored Oakland	N7277U	Boeing 727-222		*City of Cleveland*
N7252U	Boeing 727-222	N7278U	Boeing 727-222	N7445U	Boeing 727-222
N7253U	Boeing 727-222	N7279U	Boeing 727-222	N7446U	Boeing 727-222
N7254U	Boeing 727-222		*Leon D. Cuddeback*	N7447U	Boeing 727-222
N7255U	Boeing 727-222	N7280U	Boeing 727-222	N7448U	Boeing 727-222
	City of Cleveland	N7281U	Boeing 727-222	N7449U	Boeing 727-222
N7256U	Boeing 727-222	N7282U	Boeing 727-222	N7450U	Boeing 727-222
N7257U	Boeing 727-222	N7283U	Boeing 727-222	N7451U	Boeing 727-222
N7258U	Boeing 727-222	N7284U	Boeing 727-222	N7452U	Boeing 727-222
N7259U	Boeing 727-222	N7285U	Boeing 727-222	N7453U	Boeing 727-222
N7260U	Boeing 727-222	N7286U	Boeing 727-222	N7454U	Boeing 727-222
N7261U	Boeing 727-222	N7287U	Boeing 727-222	N7455U	Boeing 727-222
N7262U	Boeing 727-222	N7288U	Boeing 727-222	N7456U	Boeing 727-222
N7263U	Boeing 727-222	N7289U	Boeing 727-222	N7457U	Boeing 727-222
N7264U	Boeing 727-222	N7290U	Boeing 727-222	N7458U	Boeing 727-222
N7265U	Boeing 727-222	N7291U	Boeing 727-222	N7459U	Boeing 727-222
N7266U	Boeing 727-222	N7292U	Boeing 727-222	N7460U	Boeing 727-222
N7267U	Boeing 727-222	N7293U	Boeing 727-222	N7461U	Boeing 727-222
N7268U	Boeing 727-222	N7294U	Boeing 727-222	N7462U	Boeing 727-222
N7269U	Boeing 727-222	N7295U	Boeing 727-222	N7463U	Boeing 727-222
N7270U	Boeing 727-222	N7297U	Boeing 727-222	N7464U	Boeing 727-222
N7271U	Boeing 727-222	N7298U	Boeing 727-222	N7465U	Boeing 727-222
N7272U	Boeing 727-222	N7299U	Boeing 727-222	N7466U	Boeing 727-222
N7273U	Boeing 727-222	N7441U	Boeing 727-222	N7467U	Boeing 727-222
N7274U	Boeing 727-222	N7442U	Boeing 727-222		
N7275U	Boeing 727-222	N7443U	Boeing 727-222		

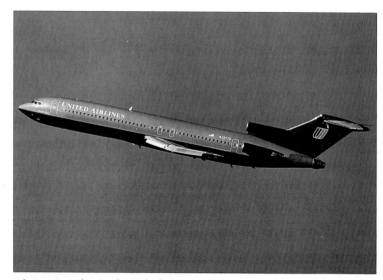

Above: *Now long in the tooth, the 727 may no longer be the 'world's favourite airliner' but it is still much in demand with many improvements — noise reduction, EFIS cockpits, two-man cockpit, etc — available.* United Airlines

Below: *727-222 N7270U at San Diego. It was delivered in 1978.* Peter R. March

Right: *Publicity photograph showing off the 737-500, the smallest airliner in the current Boeing range leading out United's 737-300 and KLM's 737-400. United would order over 60, the first being delivered in November 1990.* Boeing

Registration/Aircraft Type		Registration/Aircraft Type		Registration/Aircraft Type	
N9002U	Boeing 737-222	N302UA	Boeing 737-322	N349UA	Boeing 737-322
N9003U	Boeing 737-222	N303UA	Boeing 737-322	N350UA	Boeing 737-322
N9004U	Boeing 737-222	N304UA	Boeing 737-322	N351UA	Boeing 737-322
N9006U	Boeing 737-222	N305UA	Boeing 737-322	N352UA	Boeing 737-322
N9007U	Boeing 737-222	N306UA	Boeing 737-322	N353UA	Boeing 737-322
N9008U	Boeing 737-222	N307UA	Boeing 737-322	N354UA	Boeing 737-322
N9009U	Boeing 737-222	N308UA	Boeing 737-322	N355UA	Boeing 737-322
N9010U	Boeing 737-222	N309UA	Boeing 737-322	N356UA	Boeing 737-322
N9011U	Boeing 737-222	N310UA	Boeing 737-322	N357UA	Boeing 737-322
N9012U	Boeing 737-222	N311UA	Boeing 737-322	N358UA	Boeing 737-322
N9013U	Boeing 737-222	N312UA	Boeing 737-322	N359UA	Boeing 737-322
N9015U	Boeing 737-222	N313UA	Boeing 737-322	N360UA	Boeing 737-322
N9016U	Boeing 737-222	N314UA	Boeing 737-322	N361UA	Boeing 737-322
N9017U	Boeing 737-222	N315UA	Boeing 737-322	N362UA	Boeing 737-322
N9018U	Boeing 737-222	N316UA	Boeing 737-322	N363UA	Boeing 737-322
N9019U	Boeing 737-222	N317UA	Boeing 737-322	N364UA	Boeing 737-322
N9022U	Boeing 737-222	N318UA	Boeing 737-322	N365UA	Boeing 737-322
N9023U	Boeing 737-222	N319UA	Boeing 737-322	N366UA	Boeing 737-322
N9024U	Boeing 737-222	N320UA	Boeing 737-322	N367UA	Boeing 737-322
N9025U	Boeing 737-222	N321UA	Boeing 737-322	N368UA	Boeing 737-322
N9027U	Boeing 737-222	N322UA	Boeing 737-322	N369UA	Boeing 737-322
N9030U	Boeing 737-222	N323UA	Boeing 737-322	N370UA	Boeing 737-322
N9032U	Boeing 737-222	N324UA	Boeing 737-322	N371UA	Boeing 737-322
N9038U	Boeing 737-222	N325UA	Boeing 737-322	N372UA	Boeing 737-322
N9039U	Boeing 737-222	N326UA	Boeing 737-322	N373UA	Boeing 737-322
N9040U	Boeing 737-222	N327UA	Boeing 737-322	N374UA	Boeing 737-322
N9045U	Boeing 737-222	N328UA	Boeing 737-322	N375UA	Boeing 737-322
N9051U	Boeing 737-222	N329UA	Boeing 737-322	N376UA	Boeing 737-322
N9052U	Boeing 737-222	N330UA	Boeing 737-322	N377UA	Boeing 737-322
N9053U	Boeing 737-222	N331UA	Boeing 737-322	N378UA	Boeing 737-322
N9054U	Boeing 737-222	N332UA	Boeing 737-322	N379UA	Boeing 737-322
N9060U	Boeing 737-222	N333UA	Boeing 737-322	N380UA	Boeing 737-322
N9063U	Boeing 737-222	N334UA	Boeing 737-322	N381UA	Boeing 737-322
N9065U	Boeing 737-222	N335UA	Boeing 737-322	N382UA	Boeing 737-322
N9066U	Boeing 737-222	N336UA	Boeing 737-322	N383UA	Boeing 737-322
N9067U	Boeing 737-222	N337UA	Boeing 737-322	N384UA	Boeing 737-322
N9068U	Boeing 737-222	N338UA	Boeing 737-322	N385UA	Boeing 737-322
N9069U	Boeing 737-222	N340UA	Boeing 737-322	N386UA	Boeing 737-322
N9070U	Boeing 737-222	N341UA	Boeing 737-322	N387UA	Boeing 737-322
N9071U	Boeing 737-222	N342UA	Boeing 737-322	N388UA	Boeing 737-322
N9072U	Boeing 737-222	N343UA	Boeing 737-322	N389UA	Boeing 737-322
N9075U	Boeing 737-222	N344UA	Boeing 737-322	N390UA	Boeing 737-322
		N345UA	Boeing 737-322	N391UA	Boeing 737-322
N202UA	Boeing 737-322	N346UA	Boeing 737-322	N392UA	Boeing 737-322
N203UA	Boeing 737-322	N347UA	Boeing 737-322	N393UA	Boeing 737-322
N301UA	Boeing 737-322	N348UA	Boeing 737-322	N394UA	Boeing 737-322

Above: *Boeing 737-222 N9075U was delivered in 1969.*

Registration/Aircraft Type		Registration/Aircraft Type		Registration/Aircraft Type	
N395UA	Boeing 737-322	N925UA	Boeing 737-522	N955UA	Boeing 737-522
N396UA	Boeing 737-322	N926UA	Boeing 737-522	N956UA	Boeing 737-522
N397UA	Boeing 737-322	N927UA	Boeing 737-522	N957UA	Boeing 737-522
N398UA	Boeing 737-322	N928UA	Boeing 737-522		
N399UA	Boeing 737-322	N929UA	Boeing 737-522	N974UA	Boeing 737-2A1
		N930UA	Boeing 737-522	N976UA	Boeing 737-2A1
N901UA	Boeing 737-522	N931UA	Boeing 737-522		
N902UA	Boeing 737-522	N932UA	Boeing 737-522	N977UA	Boeing 737-291
N903UA	Boeing 737-522	N933UA	Boeing 737-522	N978UA	Boeing 737-291
N904UA	Boeing 737-522	N934UA	Boeing 737-522	N979UA	Boeing 737-291
N905UA	Boeing 737-522	N935UA	Boeing 737-522	N980UA	Boeing 737-291
N906UA	Boeing 737-522	N936UA	Boeing 737-522	N981UA	Boeing 737-291
N907UA	Boeing 737-522	N937UA	Boeing 737-522	N982UA	Boeing 737-291
N908UA	Boeing 737-522	N938UA	Boeing 737-522	N983UA	Boeing 737-291
N909UA	Boeing 737-522	N939UA	Boeing 737-522	N984UA	Boeing 737-291
N910UA	Boeing 737-522	N940UA	Boeing 737-522	N985UA	Boeing 737-291
N911UA	Boeing 737-522	N941UA	Boeing 737-522	N986UA	Boeing 737-291
N912UA	Boeing 737-522	N942UA	Boeing 737-522	N987UA	Boeing 737-291
N913UA	Boeing 737-522	N943UA	Boeing 737-522	N988UA	Boeing 737-291
N914UA	Boeing 737-522	N944UA	Boeing 737-522	N989UA	Boeing 737-291
N915UA	Boeing 737-522	N945UA	Boeing 737-522	N990UA	Boeing 737-291
N916UA	Boeing 737-522	N946UA	Boeing 737-522	N991UA	Boeing 737-291
N917UA	Boeing 737-522	N947UA	Boeing 737-522	N992UA	Boeing 737-291
N918UA	Boeing 737-522	N948UA	Boeing 737-522	N993UA	Boeing 737-291
N919UA	Boeing 737-522	N949UA	Boeing 737-522	N994UA	Boeing 737-291
N920UA	Boeing 737-522	N950UA	Boeing 737-522	N995UA	Boeing 737-291
N921UA	Boeing 737-522	N951UA	Boeing 737-522	N996UA	Boeing 737-291
N922UA	Boeing 737-522	N952UA	Boeing 737-522	N997UA	Boeing 737-291
N923UA	Boeing 737-522	N953UA	Boeing 737-522	N998UA	Boeing 737-291
N924UA	Boeing 737-522	N954UA	Boeing 737-522		

Above: N147UA, a Boeing 747SP21 came from Pan Am, to whom it was delivered in 1978. United bought it and re-registered it in 1986 and it served until 1994 when it was withdrawn from service and stored. Leo Marriott

Below: 747-451 N106UA was one of two (the other being 105, 757-451S) originally destined for Northwest but not taken up. United bought it in 1994. Austin J. Brown

Registration/AircraftType		Registration/AircraftType	
N4714U	Boeing 747-122 *Justin Dart*	N163UA	Boeing 747-238B
N4716U	Boeing 747-122	N164UA	Boeing 747-238B *Shane Barnes Customer*
N4717U	Boeing 747-122 stored Las Vegas *Edward E.Carlson*	N165UA	Boeing 747-238B *Daniel J. Terra Customer*
N4718U	Boeing 747-122 *Thomas F. Gleed*	N104UA	Boeing 747-422 on order 9/97 *Rosa Santana Employee*
N4719U	Boeing 747-122 *Friendship Japan*	N171UA	Boeing 747-422 *Spirit of Seattle 2*
N4720U	Boeing 747-122	N172UA	Boeing 747-422
N4723U	Boeing 747-122 *William A. Patterson*	N173UA	Boeing 747-422
		N174UA	Boeing 747-422 *Mitch Lee Employee*
N4724U	Boeing 747-122	N175UA	Boeing 747-422
N4727U	Boeing 747-122 stored *Robert E. Johnson*	N176UA	Boeing 747-422
N4728U	Boeing 747-122 *Gardner Cowles* leased from GECC	N177UA	Boeing 747-422
		N178UA	Boeing 747-422
N4729U	Boeing 747-122	N179UA	Boeing 747-422
N4732U	Boeing 747-122	N180UA	Boeing 747-422 *Edwin D. Fuller Customer*
N4735U	Boeing 747-122	N181UA	Boeing 747-422
N153UA	Boeing 747-123	N182UA	Boeing 747-422
N154UA	Boeing 747-123	N183UA	Boeing 747-422
N155UA	Boeing 747-123	N184UA	Boeing 747-422
N156UA	Boeing 747-123	N185UA	Boeing 747-422
N157UA	Boeing 747-123	N186UA	Boeing 747-422
		N187UA	Boeing 747-422
N145UA	Boeing 747SP21 stored Las Vegas	N188UA	Boeing 747-422
N146UA	Boeing 747SP21 stored LasVegas	N189UA	Boeing 747-422 *Herkea Jea Customer*
N147UA	Boeing 747SP21 stored Marana	N190UA	Boeing 747-422
		N191UA	Boeing 747-422
N151UA	Boeing 747SP-222B	N192UA	Boeing 747-422
N152UA	Boeing 747SP-222B *Carolina Y. C. Woo Customer*	N193UA	Boeing 747-422
		N194UA	Boeing 747-422
		N195UA	Boeing 747-422
N158UA	Boeing 747-238B *E Ticket Team Employees*	N196UA	Boeing 747-422
N159UA	Boeing 747-238B *Bobbi Philips Customer*	N197UA	Boeing 747-422 on order 4/97
		N198UA	Boeing 747-422 on order
N160UA	Boeing 747-238B *Harry M. Kubetz Customer*	N199UA	Boeing 747-422 on order
N161UA	Boeing 747-238B *Michael Stears Customer*	N105UA	Boeing 747-451 *Randy Weinacht Employee*
		N106UA	Boeing 747-451

Above: *N4735U is a venerable Boeing 747-122 bought in 1973. It is seen here at San Francisco in 1978.* Ian MacFarlane

Below: *N4714U* Justin Dart *was delivered to United in November 1970. It is seen at Jonbail, Saudi Arabia. Only 167 -100s were built, the first being delivered on 13 December 1970. N4715 was United's seventh 747.* Peter R. March

Above: *N7471U 747-422 — an artist's impression.* United Airlines

Below: *The main distinguishing features between the Boeing 757/767 'twins' are fuselage width and the length of the nose. The 767 is fatter and the 757 has a much longer fuselage section forward of the wing. The underside of the nose of the 757 is flatter than that of the 767 as is shown in this dramatic picture of a United 757.* United Airlines

Above: *767-222s in United service carry 10 first, 32 second and 126 economy passengers. This is N611UA, a 767-222ER, delivered in 1982.* Leo Marriott

Below: *The -322, stretched version typically seats 10 first, 32 second and 158 economy passengers. N647UA, a 767-322ER, was delivered in 1992.* Leo Marriott

Registration/Aircraft Type	Registration/Aircraft Type	Registration/Aircraft Type
N501UA Boeing 757-222	N532UA Boeing 757-222	N563UA Boeing 757-222
N502UA Boeing 757-222	N533UA Boeing 757-222	N564UA Boeing 757-222
N503UA Boeing 757-222	N534UA Boeing 757-222	N565UA Boeing 757-222
N504UA Boeing 757-222	N535UA Boeing 757-222	N566UA Boeing 757-222
N505UA Boeing 757-222	N536UA Boeing 757-222	N567UA Boeing 757-222
N506UA Boeing 757-222	N537UA Boeing 757-222	N568UA Boeing 757-222
N507UA Boeing 757-222	N538UA Boeing 757-222	N569UA Boeing 757-222
N508UA Boeing 757-222	N539UA Boeing 757-222	N570UA Boeing 757-222
N509UA Boeing 757-222	N540UA Boeing 757-222	N571UA Boeing 757-222
N510UA Boeing 757-222	N541UA Boeing 757-222	N572UA Boeing 757-222
N511UA Boeing 757-222	N542UA Boeing 757-222	N573UA Boeing 757-222
N512UA Boeing 757-222	N543UA Boeing 757-222ER	N574UA Boeing 757-222
N513UA Boeing 757-222	N544UA Boeing 757-222ER	N575UA Boeing 757-222
N514UA Boeing 757-222	N545UA Boeing 757-222ER	N576UA Boeing 757-222
N515UA Boeing 757-222	N546UA Boeing 757-222ER	N577UA Boeing 757-222
N516UA Boeing 757-222	N547UA Boeing 757-222ER	N578UA Boeing 757-222
N517UA Boeing 757-222	N548UA Boeing 757-222ER	N579UA Boeing 757-222
N518UA Boeing 757-222	N549UA Boeing 757-222ER	N580UA Boeing 757-222
N519UA Boeing 757-222	N550UA Boeing 757-222ER	N581UA Boeing 757-222
N520UA Boeing 757-222	N551UA Boeing 757-222ER	N582UA Boeing 757-222
N521UA Boeing 757-222	N552UA Boeing 757-222ER	N583UA Boeing 757-222
N522UA Boeing 757-222	N553UA Boeing 757-222	N584UA Boeing 757-222
N523UA Boeing 757-222	N554UA Boeing 757-222	N585UA Boeing 757-222
N524UA Boeing 757-222	N555UA Boeing 757-222	N586UA Boeing 757-222
N525UA Boeing 757-222	N556UA Boeing 757-222	N587UA Boeing 757-222
N526UA Boeing 757-222	N557UA Boeing 757-222	N588UA Boeing 757-222
N527UA Boeing 757-222	N558UA Boeing 757-222	N591UA Boeing 757-222
N528UA Boeing 757-222	N559UA Boeing 757-222	N592UA Boeing 757-222
N529UA Boeing 757-222	N560UA Boeing 757-222	N593UA Boeing 757-222
N530UA Boeing 757-222	N561UA Boeing 757-222	N594UA Boeing 757-222
N531UA Boeing 757-222	N562UA Boeing 757-222	N601UA Boeing 767-222

Registration	Aircraft Type/Notes	Registration	Aircraft Type/Notes
N602UA	Boeing 767-222ER	N611UA	Boeing 767-222ER
N603UA	Boeing 767-222	N612UA	Boeing 767-222
N604UA	Boeing 767-222	N613UA	Boeing 767-222
N605UA	Boeing 767-222ER	N614UA	Boeing 767-222
	Bob Rosseau Customer	N615UA	Boeing 767-222
N606UA	Boeing 767-222ER	N617UA	Boeing 767-222
	City of Chicago	N618UA	Boeing 767-222
N607UA	Boeing 767-222ER	N619UA	Boeing 767-222
	City of Denver	N620UA	Boeing 767-222
N608UA	Boeing 767-222ER	N641UA	Boeing 767-322ER
N609UA	Boeing 767-222ER	N642UA	Boeing 767-322ER
N610UA	Boeing 767-222ER	N643UA	Boeing 767-322ER

Above: *United Airlines 777-222ER N770UA* Thomas R. Stuker Customer *showing clear nose markings and cargo loading/unloading system.* Peter R. March

Below: *United 777-222 N772UA* Mary Beth Loesch Customer. United Airlines

Registration	Aircraft Type/Notes	Registration	Aircraft Type/Notes
N644UA	Boeing 767-322ER	N654UA	Boeing 767-322ER
N645UA	Boeing 767-322ER	N655UA	Boeing 767-322ER
N646UA	Boeing 767-322ER	N656UA	Boeing 767-322ER
N647UA	Boeing 767-322ER	N657UA	Boeing 767-322ER
N648UA	Boeing 767-322ER	N658UA	Boeing 767-322ER
N649UA	Boeing 767-322ER	N659UA	Boeing 767-322ER
N650UA	Boeing 767-322ER	N660UA	Boeing 767-322ER
N651UA	Boeing 767-322ER	N661UA	Boeing 767-322ER
N652UA	Boeing 767-322ER	N662UA	Boeing 767-322ER
N653UA	Boeing 767-322ER	N663UA	Boeing 767-322ER

Above: *777-222 N770UA at London Heathrow on 8 April 1997.* Philip J. Birtles

Registration	Aircraft Type	Notes/Names
N766UA	Boeing 777-222	*Nancy J. Meyer Customer*
N767UA	Boeing 777-222	
N768UA	Boeing 777-222	*Marcello Amodeo Customer*
N769UA	Boeing 777-222	*D. Timothy Tamany Customer*
N770UA	Boeing 777-222	*Thomas R. Stuker Customer*
N771UA	Boeing 777-222	*Frank Grittith Customer*
N772UA	Boeing 777-222	*Mary Beth Loesch Customer*
N773UA	Boeing 777-222	*Richard H. Leung Customer*
N774UA	Boeing 777-222	*Greg Milano Customer*
N775UA	Boeing 777-222	*Scott A. Neumayer Customer*
N776UA	Boeing 777-222	
N777UA	Boeing 777-222	*Working Together*
N778UA	Boeing 777-222	
N779UA	Boeing 777-222	
N780UA	Boeing 777-222	
N781UA	Boeing 777-222	
N782UA	Boeing 777-222	on order 6/97
N783UA	Boeing 777-222	on order 2/97
N784UA	Boeing 777-222	on order 3/97
N785UA	Boeing 777-222	on order 3/97
N786UA	Boeing 777-222	on order 4/97
N787UA	Boeing 777-222	on order 5/97
N788UA	Boeing 777-222	on order 7/97
N789UA	Boeing 777-222	on order 8/97
N790UA	Boeing 777-222	on order 9/97
N791UA	Boeing 777-222	on order 10/97
N792UA	Boeing 777-222	on order 11/97
N793UA	Boeing 777-222	on order 12/97
N794UA	Boeing 777-222	on order 1/98
N795UA	Boeing 777-222	on order 2/98
N796UA	Boeing 777-222	on order 2/98
N797UA	Boeing 777-222	on order 5/98
N798UA	Boeing 777-222	on order 2/99
N799UA	Boeing 777-222	on order 5/99

Above: *DC-10-10 N1822U served with United for 20 years — from 1974 to 1994.* Leo Marriott

Registration	Aircraft Type	Notes
N1801U	Douglas DC-10-10	for Federal Express
N1802U	Douglas DC-10-10	for Federal Express
N1803U	Douglas DC-10-10	for Federal Express
N1806U	Douglas DC-10-10	for Federal Express
N1807U	Douglas DC-10-10	for Federal Express
N1808U	Douglas DC-10-10	for Federal Express
N1809U	Douglas DC-10-10	for Federal Express
N1810U	Douglas DC-10-10	for Federal Express
N1811U	Douglas DC-10-10	for Federal Express
N1812U	Douglas DC-10-10	for Federal Express
N1813U	Douglas DC-10-10	for Federal Express
N1814U	Douglas DC-10-10	for Federal Express
N1815U	Douglas DC-10-10	for Federal Express
N1816U	Douglas DC-10-10	for Federal Express
N1817U	Douglas DC-10-10	for Federal Express
N1818U	Douglas DC-10-10	for Federal Express

Above: *N1837U, a DC-10-10, is another destined for FedEx.* Ian MacFarlane

Registration	Aircraft Type	Notes
N1820U	Douglas DC-10-10	for Federal Express
N1821U	Douglas DC-10-10	for Federal Express
N1822U	Douglas DC-10-10	for Federal Express
N1823U	Douglas DC-10-10	for Federal Express
N1824U	Douglas DC-10-10	for Federal Express
N1825U	Douglas DC-10-10	for Federal Express
N1826U	Douglas DC-10-10	for Federal Express
N1827U	Douglas DC-10-10	for Federal Express
N1828U	Douglas DC-10-10	for Federal Express
N1829U	Douglas DC-10-10	for Federal Express
N1830U	Douglas DC-10-10	for Federal Express
N1831U	Douglas DC-10-10	for Federal Express
N1832U	Douglas DC-10-10	for Federal Express
N1833U	Douglas DC-10-10	for Federal Express
N1834U	Douglas DC-10-10	for Federal Express
N1835U	Douglas DC-10-10	for Federal Express
N1836U	Douglas DC-10-10	for Federal Express
N1837U	Douglas DC-10-10	for Federal Express
N1838U	Douglas DC-10-10	
N1839U	Douglas DC-10-10	
N1841U	Douglas DC-10-10	for Federal Express
N1842U	Douglas DC-10-10	
N1843U	Douglas DC-10-10	
N1844U	Douglas DC-10-10	
N1845U	Douglas DC-10-10	
N1846U	Douglas DC-10-10	for Federal Express
N1847U	Douglas DC-10-10	
N1849U	Douglas DC-10-10	
N1852U	Douglas DC-10 30	
N1853U	Douglas DC-10 30	
N1854U	Douglas DC-10 30	
N1855U	Douglas DC-10 30	
N1856U	Douglas DC-10 30CF	
N1857U	Douglas DC-10 30CF	
N1858U	Douglas DC-10 30CF	
N1859U	Douglas DC-10 30CF	leased from CIT

United Express (UA Feeder Lines) (UA/UAL)

United Express/Air Wisconsin (ZW/AWI)
(Main Hub — Chicago O'Hare) = 7 BAe 146 200s, 2 BAe 146 100s, 5 BAe 146 300s.

United Express/Atlantic Coast Airlines Inc (BLR Blue Ridge)
(Main Hub — Washington-Dulles) = 28 BAe Jetstream 41s (with a further 12 on order), 30 BAe Jetstream 3201s.

United Express/Great Lakes Aviation Ltd (ZK/GLA 'Lakes Air')
(Main Hub — Chicago) = 25 Beech 1900C-1s, 10 Beech 1900Ds, 14 EMB-120RT Brasilias.

United Express/Mountain West Airlines (MSE 'Air Shuttle')
(Main Hub — Denver, only certain aircraft) = 20 Beech 1900Ds, 3 EMB-120RT Brasilias, 9 DHC-8 202s and 1 DHC-8 300.

United Express/United Feeder Service
(Main Hub — Chicago O'Hare) = 9 BAe ATPs.

United Express/WestAir Commuter Airlines (OE/SDU 'Sundance')
(Main Hubs — Los Angeles, Seattle, Denver, San Francisco) = 21 BAe Jetstream 3101s, 21 EMB-120RT Brasilias.

Left: *The larges single user of Denver Int. Airport. United Airlines' aircraft dominate this line-up.* Niall Booth

Below: *F-27 Friendship which was used by Air Wisconsin from December 1985 to December 1991. Today the airline uses BAe146-200s.* Austin J. Brown

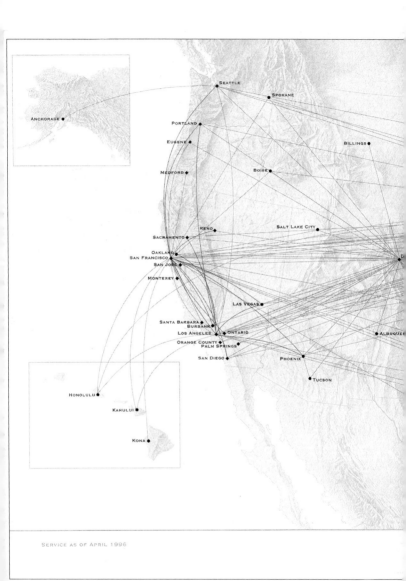

Below: *Map of United's domestic US routes.* United Airlines

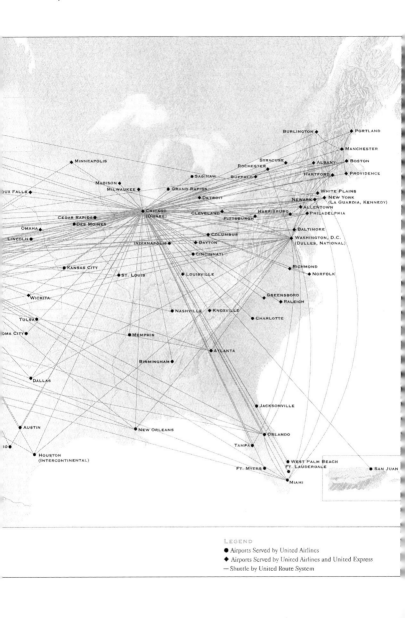

LEGEND
● Airports Served by United Airlines
◆ Airports Served by United Airlines and United Express
— Shuttle by United Route System

Engineering and Training

MAINTENANCE OPERATIONS DIVISION

To service and maintain its fleet to the highest specifications, United Airlines runs a separate division entirely devoted to looking after the mechanical side of its business. There are three principal maintenance centres at San Francisco, Oakland and the latest one, still under construction, in Indianapolis. For routine line maintenance, United in 1995 had employees at 27 domestic and 19 international centres.

INDIANAPOLIS

When completed, this facility will provide approximately 2.6 million square feet under cover. It will house 11 hangars with 18 aircraft bays and two nose bays, a state-of-the-art maintenance and repair facility, plus administrative offices and a wide range of support facilities for electronics, avionics, cleaning and machine work. By 2004 it is projected that the Indianapolis Maintenance Center will employ 7,500 people.

SAN FRANCISCO

This is the largest facility of its kind in the world, with more than three million square feet under cover, on a 144-acre site. Much of the storage, retrieval and distribution is done by high-tech industrial robots, and machining is numerically controlled. There are also multifunction repair processes. All this technology supports and supplies the service shops which in turn support state-of-the-art avionics equipment, with sophisticated hydraulic, pneumatic and electrical systems, and sheet metal, composite and interior structures.

In 1994 San Francisco carried out maintenance and special project work on 1,334 airframes. They also checked and repaired 743 engines, 4,234 modules and 345 auxiliary power units, plus 700,000 recoverable components.

OAKLAND

In 1994, 122 aircraft passed through here for various maintenance requirements and for special projects.

Below: *757-222 N523UA at Detroit. Delivered end 1990.* Peter R. March

Above: *777 cold weather testing in Sweden. The third 777, completed in August 1994, it would be delivered to United as N771UA.* Boeing

FLIGHT ATTENDANT TRAINING

United Airlines trains its flight attendants in an eight-storey complex adjacent to its world headquarters near Chicago. In 1995 more than 2,000 flight attendants were trained here, with around 500 personnel being trained at any one time.

The training programme lasts for seven weeks during which time all flight contingencies are covered. Specific service training is given on each of the types of aircraft United operates, including all safety aspects, first aid training, extensive training in dealing politely with customers, as well as cultural awareness. Much of this training is computer-based, but it also includes extensive practical lessons using a fully operational aircraft cabin simulator. An integral slice of this period is a rigorous six-day emergency procedures course which includes several training flights.

In common with flight crew, flight attendants undergo an annual recurrent training session to keep their emergency training skills at peak levels. For those who wish to fly United's vast international routes, extra courses are offered to help with the wider diversity of passenger they will meet.

DENVER FLIGHT TRAINING CENTER

In common with all the major airlines, United likes to train its own pilots in the company's own methods to its own high standards. To do this, United opened one of the largest commercial pilot training facilities in the world — 300,000sq ft in total — at the Denver Flight Training Center. Inside it contains 26 flight simulators as well as many other training devices, cockpit procedure trainers, autoflight system trainers, emergency evacuation trainers and more than 90 computer-based training stations.

In 1994 United took 137 candidate pilots for 45 days of initial training. Furthermore, every United pilot receives transition training whenever he/she is moved from one type of aircraft to another and even when moving from one seat to another in the same aircraft type. In 1995 transition training, which typically takes 30 days, was given to 1,296 pilots.

In addition, every United Airlines pilot attends annual recurrent training sessions to be kept right up to date with the latest aviation developments and to be reminded of correct systems procedures.